Doors, Windows & Skylights: Selecting & Installing

Created and Designed by the Editorial Staff of Ortho Books

Project Editor
Alan Ahlstrand

Writers
Roberto Lombardi
T. Jeff Williams

Principal Photographer
Geoffrey Nilsen

Photo Editor
Roberta Spieckerman

Principal Illustrator
Edith Allgood

W9-AZT-084

Ortho Books

Publisher
Richard E. Pile, Jr.

Editorial Director
Christine Jordan

Production Director
Ernie S. Tasaki

Managing Editors
Robert J. Beckstrom
Michael D. Smith
Sally W. Smith

System Manager
Linda M. Bouchard

Marketing Specialist
Daniel Stage

Distribution Specialist
Barbara F. Steadham

Sales Manager
Thomas J. Leahy

Technical Consultant
J. A. Crozier, Jr., Ph.D.

Address all inquiries to:
Ortho Books
Box 5047
San Ramon, CA 94583-0947

Copyright © 1984, 1992
Monsanto Company
All rights reserved under international and Pan-American copyright conventions.

6   7   8   9
        98 99

ISBN 0-89721-241-X
Library of Congress Catalog Card Number 91-73779

THE SOLARIS GROUP
2527 Camino Ramon
San Ramon, CA 94583-0906

Copy Chief
Melinda E. Levine

Editorial Coordinator
Cass Dempsey

Copyeditor
Irene Elmer

Layout by
Cynthia Putnam

Proofreader
Deborah Bruner

Indexer
Elinor Lindheimer

Editorial Assistants
John Parr
Nancy Patton Wilson

Composition by
Laurie A. Steele

Production by
Studio 165

Separations by
Color Tech Corp.

Lithographed in the USA by
Webcrafters, Inc.

Special Thanks to
Joan Annett and Ed Osborn

Front Cover Collage
Roberta Spieckerman

Front Cover 3D Modeling & Rendering
Epso Suspendo Animation

Homeowner
Maria Arapakis

Architects/Designers/Contractors
Glen Jarvis Architects: 4–5; 76–77; back cover TR
Joint Enterprises, Christopher Osborn: 4–5; back cover TR
Loretta Kelly Korch, Interior Design, Palo Alto, Calif.: front cover, column 1 top; 3; 23; 48–49; 88
The Steinberg Group, Rob Steinberg Architect, San Jose, Calif.: front cover, column 1 top; 3; 23; 48–49; 88

Manufacturers
Andersen Windows: 89
The Atrium Door and Window Company: 17
Baldwin Hardware Corp.: front cover, column 2 center; 15
Bennett Industries, Inc.: 40B; back cover BL
Borwick Innovations, Inc., Santa Barbara, Calif.: front cover, column 3 bottom; 14
Clopay Corporation: 9; back cover BR
Eagle Window and Door, Inc.: front cover, column 4 bottom; 8B; 50
Peachtree Doors and Windows: 16
Pella/Rolscreen Company: front cover, column 1 bottom; 40T; 66; 68; 81B
Simpson Door Company: front cover, column 3 center; 1
Therma-Tru Corp.: 8T; 10
VELUX-AMERICA, INC.: front cover, column 4 top; 3; 23; 48–49; 78; 81TL; 81TR; 88; back cover TL

Photographers
Names of photographers are followed by the page numbers on which their work appears.
R = right, C = center, L = left, T = top, B = bottom.

Jack Fleming: front cover, column 3 bottom; 14
Stephen Marley Productions: 74
Geoff Nilsen Photography: front cover, column 1 top; 3; 4–5; 23; 48–49; 76–77; 88; back cover TR
Said Nuseibeh: 57
Ortho Library: front cover, column 3 top; 90–91
Jim Reuter: front cover, column 3 center; 1
Ken Rice: 58, 67
Michael Sechman: front cover, column 1 center; front cover, column 2 top & bottom; front cover, column 4 center

Title Page
An entry door can provide a design statement and a unifying theme for the house. The graceful arch of the transom above these double doors is repeated in the living room passageway and the window beyond.

Page 3
This versatile window treatment, repeated throughout the house, adds visual interest and an open feeling.

Back Cover
Top left: Open to the treetops, this array of windows and skylights provides a squirrel's-eye view of the kitchen.
Top right: A French door adds light and an open feeling to this spacious entryway.
Bottom left: Doors can beautify the interior of a home as effectively as furniture and window coverings.
Bottom right: A carefully integrated display of doors and windows enhances the stately appearance of this home.

Doors, Windows & Skylights: Selecting & Installing

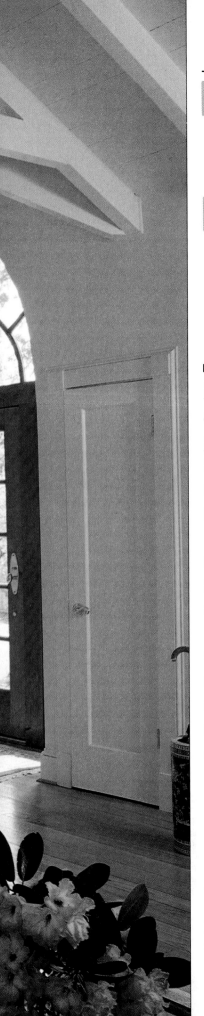

DOORS

Doors, windows, and skylights are much more than simple openings in the walls or roof. They are parts of your house that you see and touch every day. New doors, windows, and skylights can set the tone of a home; they can provide an updated look, convenient features, smooth operation, and lower energy costs.

Modern doors, windows, and skylights offer a dazzling array of improvements and new features. This book will help you to understand the new product technologies and installation methods and to choose the ones that best meet your needs.

This chapter tells how to plan the installation of doors and where and how to shop for them. It also shows how, with basic carpentry skills, you can install doors yourself. The second chapter focuses on windows, and the third chapter discusses skylights. Detailed information on maintenance and repair of doors, windows, and skylights is presented in the fourth chapter.

An unusual but effective entry-door treatment, this French door is accented
by its paned sidelights and fan-shaped transom. Wood stair railings and
newel posts help the door blend into the entryway.

DESIGN AND PLANNING

When you replace or install doors, plan ahead. It is tempting to get right to the fun of buying the doors and hanging them, but careful attention to planning will make the job go more smoothly.

Setting the Tone

The front door is an introduction to the home; it can set or change the tone of the whole house. A traditional paneled door, for instance, gives a more formal look. If you want a country accent, how about an informal Dutch door or a French door?

Be careful, however, to understand the limits of this approach. It is important to work with the existing style of the house, so that the new doors harmonize with the rest. The wrong door can be more of an eyesore than an improvement. A common mistake is to fall in love with a certain style of door without considering whether it is appropriate for your home. For instance, a metal sliding glass door does not complement Victorian architecture, and paneled interior doors may look completely out of place in a contemporary home. Occasionally a contrasting style, used in moderation, can be striking, but generally speaking, in planning for new doors it's best to maintain consistency of design.

Circulation

If you are replacing doors, aesthetics and functionality are the main concerns, but if you are planning to install a new door, you must consider circulation. The location of the door will affect the traffic pattern through the room. Consider that effect carefully. Will furniture have to be moved? How about floor coverings? Remember too that the light switches should be near the entrance to the room.

Exterior Doors

Consider weather resistance and security in planning an exterior door.

Weather

Exterior doors must be weather resistant. Wind, rain, and snow will all pass through an open door as easily as people, unless you take precautions to keep them out. In cold or windy climates, it's best to avoid any new installation that faces the prevailing wind. If this is impossible, and if there is room inside the house, consider shielding the entry from direct blasts of wind with a wall. Even a half-wall can be helpful, since cold air will sink.

If driving wind and rain are a problem, plan for a sheltering roof of some kind over the door. Be sure to include a rain gutter or diverter so you won't have to walk through a waterfall to get to the door. If wind is

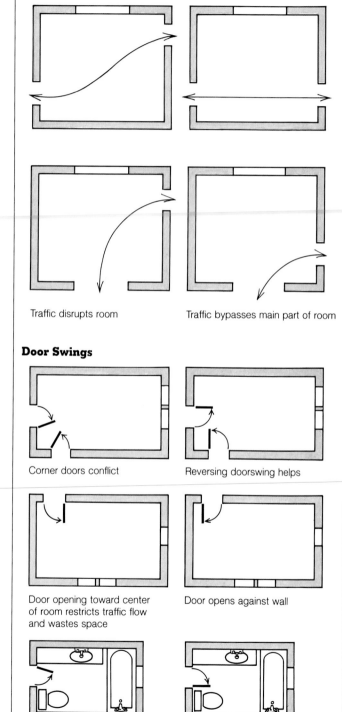

Factors to Consider in Planning Door Locations and Swings

Door Locations Affect Traffic Flow

Traffic disrupts room

Traffic bypasses main part of room

Door Swings

Corner doors conflict

Reversing doorswing helps

Door opening toward center of room restricts traffic flow and wastes space

Door opens against wall

Door opens against sink, minimizes privacy

Door provides easy access to sink, maximizes privacy

Door Styles

Entry door with transparent panels

Entry door with sidelights

Dutch door

Double sliding French doors with transom

Double entry doors with transom and sidelights

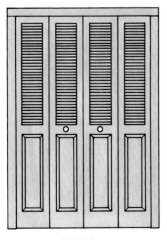

Bifold doors

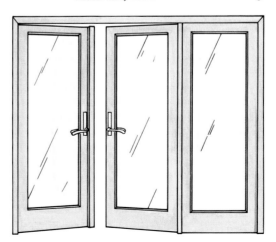

Three-piece patio door with double door and fixed panel

the main problem, try to plan for an exterior wall to one side of the door, or across the front a short distance away. Be creative with the wind screening and make whatever you build into an attractive feature. A masonry wall or a wood fence can have a decorative design that complements the door and the overall look of the house. In warmer parts of the country, you may be able to block the wind with a trellis and some well-established vines.

A good overhanging roof above the door will also help to protect it from weathering and from leaking. Doors are designed to be water- and wind resistant, but they are not waterproof. Allowing water to stream over a door is inviting trouble. Try to prevent water damage through good planning and design.

Light and Ventilation

Exterior doors can also be used to bring light and air into a room. French doors and sliding glass doors both admit plenty of light, but French doors are harder to screen than sliding doors. For the look of a traditional French door with the convenience of easy screening, consider wood sliding doors.

Security

Where security is a concern, exterior doors should be equipped with dead bolts. Metal doors are strong and fire resistant. Solid wood doors are also secure, but check paneled doors carefully. Sometimes the panels are thin and easy to break through. Avoid front-door units with

small sidelight windows, unless the sidelights are made of a breakage-resistant plastic. Otherwise a burglar could smash a window and reach in for the doorknob. If the door itself has transparent or translucent panels, they too should be made of breakage-resistant material.

French doors and sliding glass doors pose some problems. The older metal sliding doors were notoriously easy to jimmy. Some units could be opened simply by lifting out one panel, especially in cases where the movable panel was mounted on the outer side of the door unit. Make sure this can't be done with any new door you buy. Inspect the locking mechanism of the door carefully, and choose a model with security features, such as throw bolts. Make sure the latch is solidly made and that it closes securely. If you are worried about the glass being

Doors made of modern materials (top: fiberglass; bottom: steel) give the appearance of traditional wood-paneled units but offer increased insulation, fire resistance, and security.

broken, remember that a large piece of tempered glass makes a tremendous noise when it breaks. This may provide additional safety, depending on the proximity of neighbors and on

how often you are home. In the case of multilight French doors, consider breakage-resistant glazing. Finally, any door can be outfitted with a burglar alarm.

Safety

Check the local code requirements for the use of tempered glass in and around door openings. Tempered glass is heat treated to break into tiny fragments instead of dangerous, large shards. New doors almost always come with tempered glass, but be sure to replace the old glass if you buy an antique or salvaged door. Most building codes generally require that window glass within 18 inches of a door be tempered as well. You should also install tempered glass in any window that might be struck by a swinging door.

Some building codes restrict the placement of door or window openings along certain property lines. These rules generally affect older homes that are built very close together. Their purpose is to limit the spread of fire from one structure to another. The rules vary, and sometimes certain types of doors or windows are allowed. Again, the wisest course is to consult the local building code or fire department for more information.

Garage Doors

In planning a garage door, think first about exposure and protection from the elements. A garage door can be sheltered only from the outside. Windbreak fences, walls to the side of the door, or a small overhanging roof can provide cover.

Garage doors were traditionally made out of wood, but metal garage doors have gained in popularity. They are particularly useful where the door is exposed to severe weather or humidity, since they do not warp or swell. However, they are noisier in operation than wood doors, so before you buy one, check out an installed metal door, to make sure that the noise won't bother you.

It is almost impossible to tell the difference between metal and wood garage doors by their appearance. There are many styles to choose from; pick one that will harmonize with the architecture of the house.

Garage doors come in various widths. Different sizes of doors require different structural approaches. The wider the garage, the more combinations of door widths you can choose from. If the garage is wide enough for two vehicles, you can use two single-width doors or one double-width door. With a three-car garage, you can use a double-width door with a single-width door, or three single-width doors.

Don't forget to consider a garage door with windows. You may want to provide more natural light in the garage. You don't have to restrict yourself to rectangular windows, either. Fanciful and decorative shapes are also available.

Interior Doors

As with exterior doors, the style of the inside doors can be used to accentuate or change the mood of the house. A tremendous variety of interior doors is available, but try to maintain consistency. Too many different styles in the same house will be jarring.

Clearance

Sliding doors are often used where limited clearance precludes the use of a conventional door. Pocket doors are very popular, but in planning for one remember that the installation involves opening a hole in the wall that is about twice the size of the door. The technique is described on page 43.

Bifold and sliding doors are convenient for closets, pantries, laundries, and so forth. Sliding doors are usually fine for closets, but bifolds are preferable for laundries, because they leave the entire opening clear. Be sure to make the opening wide enough so that the folded doors clear the fronts of the appliances completely. Otherwise you may have clearance problems with a front-loading dryer, some of which have full-width doors.

Other Considerations

Consider sound when you plan an interior installation. Many interior doors are hollow on the inside, and they don't block noise as well as solid doors. This may be important if the door in question leads to a laundry room or family room. If you are replacing or adding a door between a living space and a garage, you should use a fire-resistant unit with an automatic closure device. In some areas the local building code may specify this type of door.

The fan-shaped light panels in this roll-up garage door complement the curved transom windows in the house, helping to create a unified design.

There have been almost as many innovations in retailing as there have been in door technology. One of the best is that sellers now display a large number of doors rather than relying on catalogs. It's much easier for most people to choose doors they can actually see.

Where to Shop for Doors

The traditional purchase point for doors is the local lumberyard. The selection will vary widely, as will the accessibility of the merchandise. Some lumberyards have display areas, but others, particularly those which cater largely to professional builders, may have the doors buried "over in building C, behind the plywood."

Lumberyards have been going through major marketing changes in response to the growth of home-improvement centers and door stores. You will have to check them out individually. Some offer more to the home consumer; others concentrate on professional builders. Generally speaking, lumberyard clerks are knowledgeable about the doors they stock and will be able to answer your questions.

One popular innovation is the large home-improvement center. Some of these stores concentrate on building products; others offer a wide variety of consumer products but may still carry a large selection of doors. One advantage of shopping at a home-improvement center is that all of the doors they carry will be on display, and you can take your time looking them over. Home-improvement centers compete mainly on price. If they stock something you like, they may be a good bet. Special-ordering (if it includes a service charge) will decrease your savings. Home-improvement centers often have everything in stock that you need, so that you can get it immediately instead of having to wait for delivery.

Another new development is the store that sells only the doors (and usually the windows) of one particular manufacturer. It is often a fancy showroom with fully mocked-up displays. You can expect top-notch service from well-trained salespeople at these stores. They usually offer field assistance if you run into installation problems, and some manufacturers actually provide service for the lifetime of the door—if it should need new weather stripping, for example. The only drawbacks are that this excellent service is expensive, and that the stores carry only one product line.

Stores that specialize in doors but sell more than one brand offer a bit more choice and a wider price range. Staff should be knowledgeable, but service will vary. Some of these stores do warranty work; others will refer you to the manufacturer.

Businesses that salvage or recycle building materials are great fun to visit. You can learn a lot about traditional door design and construction, and in the process you may find some treasures for your home. People who run these businesses are usually very enthusiastic, and they will be happy to answer your questions.

Traditional appearance and modern weather resistance are combined in these fiberglass patio doors, which look like wood French doors.

Don't restrict your shopping exclusively to stores. If you are in the market for doors, open your eyes to the doors you go through every day. Notice the doors in your friends' houses. You can also visit model homes and open houses to see what local builders are using. If you see something you like, the builder will usually be glad to tell you where the doors were purchased. You might find another good place to shop this way.

Visiting bed-and-breakfast inns or small hotels may lead to interesting discoveries. Many of these establishments are refurbished older buildings with the latest in doors and windows.

Materials and Construction

The material of choice for doors has traditionally been wood. People appreciate the warmth and character of wood doors. Many modern ones combine old-fashioned good looks with new materials and features designed to make them more durable, more energy efficient, and easier to operate and maintain.

The traditional solid wood paneled door is usually made up of vertical side pieces, called stiles, and horizontal members, called rails. The spaces in between are filled by the panels. The parts are glued together and are reinforced by some type of doweling or by a mortise-and-tenon system. The number of stiles and rails varies with the design of the door. If you are shopping for an exterior door, make sure that the panels are substantial enough

to provide adequate security. This is less of an issue with interior doors.

Cladding

Manufacturers add weather resistance and durability to their doors by sheathing, or cladding, them with aluminum or vinyl. Cladding is used on the exterior only. The interior is unclad, so that you can still enjoy the natural beauty of the wood.

Claddings are available in a wide variety of colors. The wood on the inside surface of the door is usually left natural by the factory. Many manufacturers treat the wood parts of their doors with a light, clear preservative coating, over which you can apply stain or paint.

Vinyl cladding or aluminum? Some manufacturers swear by only one type; others offer both. Aluminum will generally look crisper and may take paint finishes better, although your best bet is to stick with the factory colors. Vinyl is superior to aluminum in marine climates, where the salt air may pit the aluminum in time.

Other Finishes

Another protective coat for wood doors is a polyurea finish, similar to a paint but much more durable. These coatings are salt resistant, and they stretch with the wood as it swells and contracts in response to changes in temperature and humidity. This may be the answer if you object to the appearance of vinyl or aluminum cladding. Some units are available with clad jambs and a polyurea finish on the

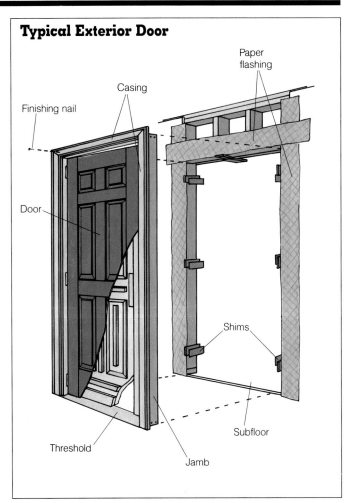

Typical Exterior Door

Paper flashing

Casing

Finishing nail

Door

Threshold

Jamb

Shims

Subfloor

door itself. This is an attractive and durable combination.

Other Materials

There are also complete alternatives to wood. In many parts of the country, steel is commonly used for exterior doors. It has the advantages of being very durable, warp-proof, non-sticking, fire resistant, secure, and thanks to insulation fillings, energy efficient. If you are not familiar with steel doors, you may be surprised at how attractive they can be.

Aluminum is generally used in sliding doors. Plain aluminum finishes, called mill finishes, are being replaced by a

very wide selection of durable painted factory finishes.

Fiberglass is another alternative to wood. Fiberglass, like metal, resists weathering, warping, and sticking. Some fiberglass doors will also accept stains and can be finished much like a wood door. Fiberglass doors are good in high-moisture locations, such as a sauna, spa, or pool house. They won't be affected by the water.

Plastics such as polyvinyl chloride (PVC) are also being used in doors. These doors, like fiberglass doors, are unaffected by damp climates or wet locations. They are durable but difficult to paint.

Anatomy of a Prehung Door

One-piece Jamb

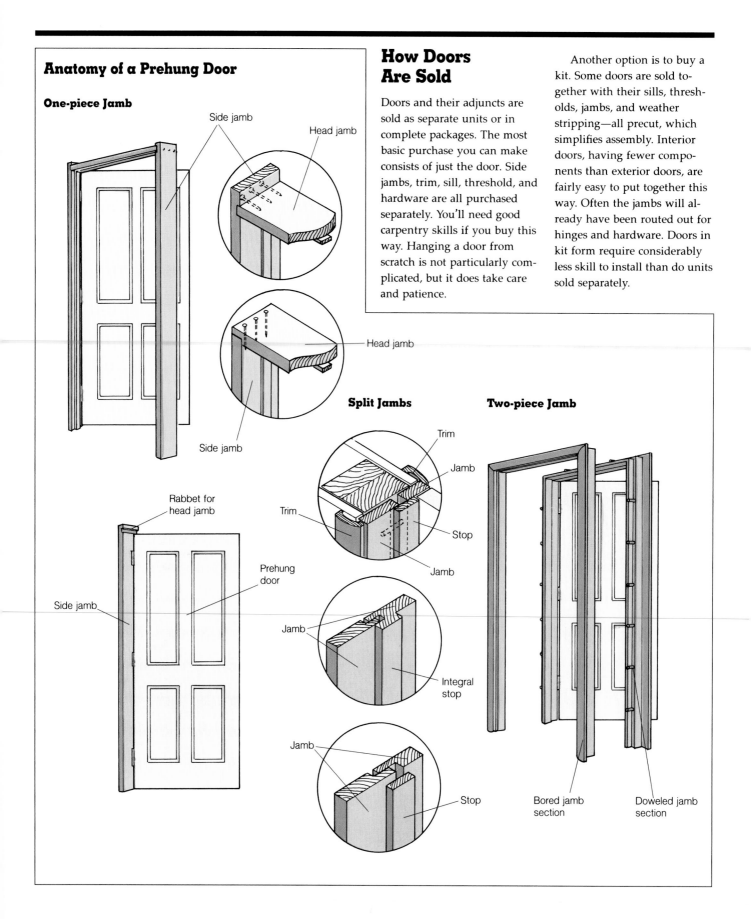

Side jamb

Head jamb

Head jamb

Side jamb

Rabbet for head jamb

Side jamb

Prehung door

Split Jambs

Trim

Jamb

Trim

Stop

Jamb

Jamb

Integral stop

Jamb

Stop

Two-piece Jamb

Bored jamb section

Doweled jamb section

How Doors Are Sold

Doors and their adjuncts are sold as separate units or in complete packages. The most basic purchase you can make consists of just the door. Side jambs, trim, sill, threshold, and hardware are all purchased separately. You'll need good carpentry skills if you buy this way. Hanging a door from scratch is not particularly complicated, but it does take care and patience.

Another option is to buy a kit. Some doors are sold together with their sills, thresholds, jambs, and weather stripping—all precut, which simplifies assembly. Interior doors, having fewer components than exterior doors, are fairly easy to put together this way. Often the jambs will already have been routed out for hinges and hardware. Doors in kit form require considerably less skill to install than do units sold separately.

Doors are also available in entirely prehung packages. Interior doors are installed in the rough opening and then trimmed out. Exterior doors come complete with a sill and may be either installed with nailing fins or nailed on through the trim.

Nailing Fins and Trim

Aluminum sliding doors, aluminum-clad wood doors, and vinyl-clad wood doors all have a flat fin about 1½ inches wide that goes around the top and sides of the door. When the door is installed in the rough opening, the fin lies flat against the exterior wall and is nailed to it, securing the entire door unit to the building. Trim or siding is then installed over the fin. Some unclad prehung wood doors, generally those which come with painted or polyurea finishes, already have exterior trim mounted on the jambs. The door is installed by nailing through the trim into the wall. The advantage here is that once you install the door, you're done. Some manufacturers offer different styles of trim on doors of this second type—for instance, 1 by 6s or traditional brick or stucco molding.

Drilling and Routing

Whether a door is sold separately, in kit form, or complete, note carefully whether it is predrilled for locksets and dead bolts and routed out for hinges. This is very important if your hardware is unusual. Most door hardware is fairly standard, but it's best to have the hardware picked out when you order the door, to make sure that it will fit. Be especially careful about

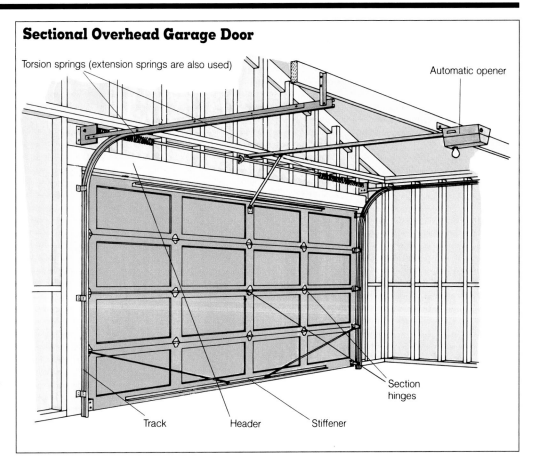

Sectional Overhead Garage Door

Torsion springs (extension springs are also used)

Automatic opener

Section hinges

Track   Header   Stiffener

fitting the hardware on metal doors, which are difficult to cut, drill, or patch.

If you plan to use antique or recycled doors, they will often be drilled or mortised for old hardware. You may have to patch or fill the existing holes, or you may be able to find hardware that fits them. If you are purchasing an old door, make certain that it is straight. Check the sides with a 6-foot level or some string stretched taut. You should also check the door diagonally.

Garage Doors

The two most popular kinds of garage doors are sectional units and swing-down units.

Both types are mounted overhead. Some garage doors are made of wood; others have wood frames with hardboard panel inserts, which will not shrink or crack.

Metal garage doors are popular and practical. They will not stick, crack, or warp, and they are available in attractive patterns. Some of them have polystyrene cores and polyethylene thermal breaks to cut heat loss.

If economy is important kits are available that consist of an unassembled steel frame, which, combined with a few sheets of plywood siding, can be used to build an attractive swing-down door.

Garage door openers also sport many features. Some can be programmed to turn on

lights elsewhere in the house. Modern openers have safety features to prevent the door from closing on a person or an object. In some systems the door senses resistance and automatically reverses. Other systems shine a beam across the door opening. If the beam is interrupted while the door is coming down, it automatically goes back up. Signal blocking is another handy feature; it lets you turn off the opener from the car. This prevents the door from being actuated by stray radio waves.

The opening mechanisms themselves are usually screw- or chain-driven. Manufacturers make various claims about the superiority of their systems; the quality of the product is probably

13

more important than which system they use. Because of the stiff competition for sales, most home-improvement centers have an entire section devoted to garage doors, openers, and accessories. Try to deal with a place that can answer your questions knowledgeably. Most of the major door and opener companies have 800 number hot lines that you can call if you have questions about their products.

Basement Doors

Years ago, the basement door was assembled on-site by the house carpenters. Today you can have the opening to the stairs measured for a fabricated steel door. These have the advantages of lightness, strength, and durability.

Pet Doors

Most of these are designed to be installed in an existing door. Pet doors come in different sizes; the commonest type consists of two frames, one for each side of the house door. The frames overlap each other to conceal the cut. This type works best in a smooth-faced door, since raised panels may cause problems with fit. It can also be installed in an exterior wall, but you will have to make your own wood side jambs to trim out the cut. The door itself consists of a heavy flap that the animal can push aside on its way in or out. The opening can be closed off with a solid door that slides down over the inside face of the pet door.

Another type of pet door is designed for use with aluminum sliding doors. It consists of a panel that is permanently installed in the sliding-door track. The panel is adjustable to fit the height of the door and includes a pet door at the bottom. After it is installed, the sliding door closes against it instead of against the side jamb.

Hardware

Many of the places that sell doors also sell hardware. Door hardware includes locksets, handles, dead bolts, hinges, and accessories such as knockers and mail slots. Some complete door units come with hardware, but you must usually choose it separately. Shop in several stores to get a good idea of what is available. Some suppliers carry only one major brand. Home-improvement centers tend to carry the less expensive lines; lumberyards and hardware stores carry lines with a wider price range. There are also stores that specialize in decorative hardware for the home, including door hardware.

For special items find a store that can special-order or that has a very wide selection. One example of such an item is a lockset with split trim, that is, with different trim on each side of the door. You might use split trim in a bathroom with chrome fixtures to give the job a professional look. That way you could have matching chrome trim on the bathroom side of the door, and brass trim on the outside of the door, to match the finishes in the rest of the house.

There are wide differences in the quality of door hardware. The most economical lines are perfectly serviceable but may come in only a few styles. As you go up in price, you should expect to see better finishes, solid as opposed to plated brass, more durability, and a better "feel." The mechanisms in high-end locksets work very smoothly, and a solid-brass handle feels much more substantial than a hollow one.

Choose hardware that is appropriate to the house. Look for a quality level and finish that match or approximate what is already there. If you want a different style, consider changing all the locksets in the house, in both the new and the old doors. If you are on a budget, consider spending more for the front-door hardware and being more economical with the interior doors. The front door is important—it is used a lot and serves as the introduction to your home. Quality here will be much seen, used, and enjoyed.

Locksets

When you shop for locksets, you'll run across the term *backset*. This refers to the distance from the centerline of the lockset to the edge of the door. The most common backset is 2⅜ inches. Other sizes are available. For wide, stately doors, choose a longer backset, which places the handles of the lockset closer to the center of the door. Beware of narrow stiles on paneled doors or French doors. It can be very expensive to get hardware that is designed for a less-than-2⅜-inch backset. Keep in mind that the 2⅜-inch measurement is to the centerline of the handle.

This pet door, which can be mounted directly into a screen, allows pets access while keeping out insects.

There must still be enough room for the rosette (the trim around the handle) to fit on the stile without overlapping the panel or the glass. This is crucial if you are building doors yourself, or if you have fallen in love with recycled doors from an older building.

The hardware in those old doors was usually installed by mortising the door to receive the lock. Mortise locks are rectangular, and a rectangular pocket (mortise) was cut in the edge of the door for the mechanism to slide into. Today some front-door locksets are mortise types, but most exterior and almost all interior locksets are round. They are installed by drilling a large hole through the face of the door and a smaller hole through the edge. This task requires a minimum of skill. Locksets come with very clear instructions, and you can even buy a kit that includes the appropriate drill bits. If the doors are predrilled, so much the better; all you'll need is a screwdriver.

Interior locksets are either the passage type or the privacy type. A passage set is used where a lock is not needed. The locks on the privacy sets are intended for very light duty. Modern units have some provision for unlocking the door in an emergency, such as a bathtub fall. Usually this is a small hole in the knob through which a nail can be pushed to unlock the door.

Security

Think about security when you choose exterior-door hardware. Keep your choice in line with the type of door you are outfitting. For instance, there is not much point in putting a heavy locking system on a single-pane French door, since it is easy to break the glass to reach the interior knob.

Some people who have glass in their doors will get a dead bolt with a key on each side, so that someone who breaks the glass can't reach in to unlock the door. Don't be tempted to do this. In case of a fire, you could be trapped in the house. Many local codes prohibit such installations.

The strongest defense against forced entry through a door is a high-quality dead-bolt lock. The dead bolt cannot be pried back once it is in the locked position. Several manufacturers of door hardware sell dead bolts finished to match the doorknobs. They also sell combination dead-bolt locksets for front doors.

The weak point of dead-bolt installations is almost always the strike hardware and jamb. Some dead bolts do not come with adequate jamb strike hardware. If the decorative strike plate is used alone, with screws that project only into the doorjamb, the door will be susceptible to forced entry, because the dead bolt will break the jamb if the door is forced open. Better dead bolts come with a strike reinforcement. This is a steel plate that sits just under the decorative brass strike on the jamb. It should be attached with screws that are long enough to penetrate well into the trimmer (the piece of wall framing directly behind the jamb). This usually means screws at least 3 inches long. For greater security longer strike reinforcement plates, attached with more screws, are available.

Be aware that a hinged door that swings outward can be opened by taking the pins out of the hinges. To prevent this, hinges are available that have a small stud, projecting from the surface of one hinge leaf, which fits into a corresponding hole in the other leaf when the door is closed. This keeps the door closed if the pins are removed.

Make sure that sliding doors have some mechanism to prevent them from being opened by lifting them out of their tracks. You can buy retrofit devices for this purpose.

Keyless locking systems, which have long been used in commercial buildings, are now available for houses. They function much like a combination lock. The owner selects the combination, which usually consists of three numbers that appear in an illuminated display. The numbers are changed by turning either a special ring or the doorknob, depending on the model. The combination can be reset temporarily to admit house sitters or service people and then changed back to its original setting.

Keyless systems can easily be installed in place of conventional door locks without special tools.

When you select door hardware, make sure that it will work with the swing of your door. The unit shown here includes a reversible latch that will work with either right- or left-hand doors.

Purchasing Doors

There is more to buying a door than just paying for it. Availability is one important issue. Special-ordering always entails risk. Be wise and realistic. Sometimes the sales staff promises delivery dates that are too optimistic just to get a sale. Make it clear to the salesperson that you will be very disappointed with an unwarranted delay. Pay particular attention to this if you are purchasing the doors for installation by a contractor. Delaying the construction crew can be costly. If you place a special order, call regularly to check on its progress.

Be certain that you have covered all of the details. Don't sign a sales order until you have had a chance to check it out carefully; if you can have someone else check it too, so

Some doors, such as this steel-surfaced entry model, come with factory finishes. Others require painting or finishing. Check the manufacturer's literature to see what's needed, and have any necessary paint or finish on hand when the door arrives.

much the better. If you see any symbols or codes you don't understand, ask what they mean. Check that the door swings are correct, that the finishes are the ones you want, that the door is predrilled for the right hardware and hinges, and that the proper glass (if any) has been installed. Make sure that the metal edge strip that divides double-pane glass is the right color, too.

If you are working with a contractor, it may be advantageous to buy the doors yourself rather than have the contractor do it. However, if you buy the doors and there is a mistake in the way they are ordered, you will be responsible for straightening it out.

The heavy marketing competition in building supplies means that there is no longer a consistent pricing policy in the industry. In the past builders and architects received a substantial price break. Today the price depends on where you shop. Generally, builders still enjoy a discount at lumberyards and other suppliers, but at discount outlets pricing may be the same for builders and homeowners. Some outfits will discount based on volume. The bigger your order, the better deal you should be able to get. Financing is offered at some places, but you might not get as good a break on the price as you would if you paid in cash.

It is reasonable for a supplier to ask for a down payment to place the order, but try to avoid paying in full unless you pick up the doors when

you pay. If there is a problem with the order later, you will have less leverage in getting it solved if the supplier already has full payment. You may also get poorer service on exchanges and returns. The bottom line is *don't pay in full until you are sure that your order is correct and undamaged.*

Delivery

Careful coordination and planning will ensure a smooth delivery day. Be sure to ask the supplier whether or not a helper for the driver will be available. Some companies have a policy of delivering materials only to the sidewalk; it may be your responsibility to get the doors into the house. Be sure to ask. *Never* schedule a delivery for a time when you cannot be there yourself. If the driver shows up alone, you will have to be his or her helper for the unloading. Line up one or two other people to help out. Try to get helpers who are both strong and careful. It's easy to damage doors by banging them into things, and it's also easy to damage the interior surfaces of the house. Don't allow anyone with a bad back to carry the doors (this includes you). Prehung door units can be extremely heavy and awkward to handle.

Check the delivery for correctness, completeness, and damage. Of course you did not pay in full before the delivery. Do not write a check for the balance now until you are certain that everything is in order. Don't let the driver pressure you into unloading quickly and paying him (or her) in full because he has to get somewhere. If he is in a hurry, tell him that you'll mail in the check, or offer partial payment. Finally, save yourself frustration by confirming the delivery time, not just the day before, but also again on the scheduled morning. Sometimes trucks break down or employees get sick. It's no fun to take a day off from work to wait for a delivery that never arrives.

Storage

Proper storage cannot be over-emphasized. Find the manufacturer's instructions for storage immediately and follow them to the letter. Typical instructions will tell you to keep the doors out of the elements. Unpainted wood doors require the greatest care. Very often they come with instructions to paint them immediately. Clad units and metal or fiberglass are less sensitive to weather. If possible, store doors or door units indoors.

Never lay doors flat for storage. They should always be leaned vertically against a flat surface. Avoid leaning them so that they are supported by only one point, or leaning them against sharp or rough surfaces. It is a good idea to cover them with a tarp or drop cloth and then lean some plywood in front, if they are going to be stored for a while.

Remember: If you don't follow the manufacturer's storage instructions, you may void the warranty—so read carefully.

With a total width of only 36 inches, these double French doors and their matching transom add visual appeal to an ordinary single doorway. Be sure to specify whether you want the doors to swing inward or outward.

STRUCTURAL PREPARATIONS

Now that the shopping and delivery are done, it's time to hoist tool belt and saw and to prepare the openings for the new doors. It will seem less intimidating to cut a hole in a wall if you break the task down into small parts, and if you know what to expect.

Anatomy of a Wall

Knowing how the typical wall is constructed will help you to understand the process of installing doors. It will also help you to understand how to alter openings, build a new wall, or temporarily support an existing one.

The basic framework of the house consists of stud walls. They are usually made of 2 by 4 lumber, although some houses have 2 by 6s. In building or altering walls, use properly graded lumber, stamped *Stud grade, Standard and better,* or *No. 2 and better.* Building codes forbid the use of cheaper and weaker grades of lumber.

The stud wall consists of the soleplate or bottom plate, which, as you would expect, is at the bottom; of vertical members called studs; and of two members at the top, called the top plate and the cap plate, or simply the double top plate. For strength, joints in the double-top-plate assembly should be offset from one another by at least 4 feet.

Studs are generally laid out on 16-inch centers, but 24-inch centers are not uncommon. When using 24-inch centers you must be sure that any joists or rafters that rest on the double top plate line up precisely over the studs. With 16-inch centers this is unnecessary. These stud spacings allow for proper placement of 4-foot-wide exterior plywood and interior wallboard or paneling; as you nail the sheets up, the edges will always fall on a stud.

Typically, wall framing is constructed with 16-penny (16d) nails. However, you may run into some interesting-looking hardware while altering a wall, particularly in parts of the country where houses are built with special attention to resisting earthquakes or wind. Members may be nailed together with framing anchors—heavy sheet-metal devices that provide more holding power than regular nails. You may also see what looks like a heavy threaded rod, typically from ½ inch to ¾ inch in diameter, running vertically through the wall or attached to a stud, a pair of studs, or a post in the wall. This is part of a hold-down assembly. It is beyond the scope of this book to explain hold-downs in

Typical Stud Wall

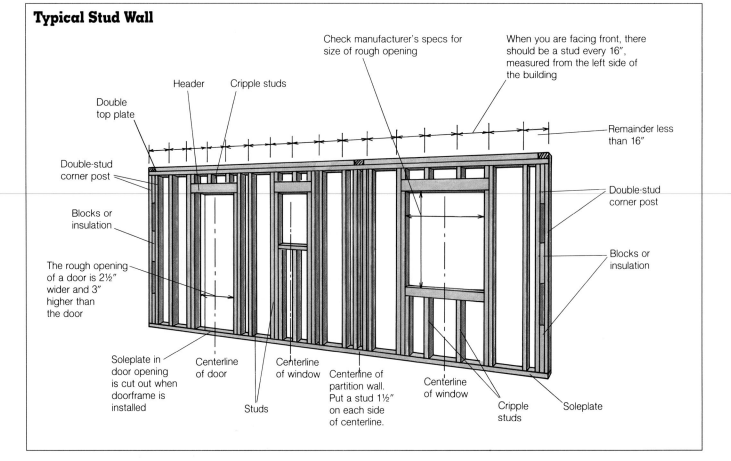

Check manufacturer's specs for size of rough opening

When you are facing front, there should be a stud every 16", measured from the left side of the building

Header

Cripple studs

Double top plate

Double-stud corner post

Remainder less than 16"

Double-stud corner post

Blocks or insulation

The rough opening of a door is 2½" wider and 3" higher than the door

Blocks or insulation

Soleplate in door opening is cut out when doorframe is installed

Centerline of door

Centerline of window

Centerline of partition wall. Put a stud 1½" on each side of centerline.

Centerline of window

Cripple studs

Soleplate

Studs

detail, but removing one without consulting an engineer could weaken the seismic or wind resistance of the house. Seek professional help if you discover a hold-down right where you were hoping to put a door. You may also run across wires, pipes, heating ducts, and so forth. To learn how to deal with these, see pages 21 to 22.

Wherever a door or window opening exists, there will be no studs to carry the load coming down from the floors or roofs above it. To support this weight a wooden member called a header is installed. Headers may be made from built-up 2-by lumber placed on edge, or they may be solid-wood beams. If you construct them, sandwich a piece of ⅜-inch plywood between two pieces of lumber. For 2 by 6 walls, you can also use solid-wood headers, or you can build up a header in slightly different form using 2-by members on edge, with 2-by or plywood top and bottom pieces. In other words, you create a kind of box beam. (Don't forget to insulate inside the header if it is hollow.)

Headers must be of an adequate size to support the weight that they carry. For practical purposes this means no sagging. Use the following table as a guide for sizing headers in a one-story house. For multistory houses, or houses

that have unusual structural features, check the local building code or consult a professional builder or an engineer.

Opening	Header Size
Up to 4' across	2 × 4s
Up to 6' across	2 × 6s
Up to 8' across	2 × 8s
Up to 10' across	2 × 10s
Up to 12' across	2 × 12s

If there is a space between the top of the header and the bottom of the double top plate, it must be filled in with studs on the same spacing as the rest of the wall. Sometimes the space may only be a few inches high, and short studs would split. In that case, simply use a bigger header. Feel free to shim the top or bottom of the header with lumber or plywood strips as necessary, just so long as there is no gap. Be sure the solid part of the header is of the required depth.

You may notice on some construction sites that the headers are all the same size and are all made out of 4 by 12s. This is done to save time on production jobs where the labor to build up headers is more expensive than the cost of solid wood. If you are doing your own work, it may be more economical to build up headers.

The headers themselves are supported at each end by trimmer (or jack) studs. The full-length studs adjacent to the ends of the header and the trimmer studs are called king studs. In some jurisdictions double trimmer studs may be

required. This applies especially in earthquake country, when openings are wider than 5 or 6 feet, or when the header carries an exceptional load.

Window openings also have a rough sill, held up by short cripple studs. In some parts of the country, rough sills are always doubled; in others they need be doubled only when the sill exceeds a certain width. Refer to the local code.

For many years in the United States, buildings were framed by the balloon method. Balloon framing has been uncommon for some time now. Most houses today are framed by the platform method. See pages 18, 24, and 25 for a discussion of both methods.

Permits and Codes

Before you make any structural changes to the house, find out whether you need a building permit. Most cities and counties require a permit for the work necessary to create new door openings. You probably won't need a permit simply to replace old doors, using the existing frames. Check with the local county or city government to find out how to contact the appropriate building department.

The building department will require specific information from you before it will issue a permit. Save yourself from having to redo the plans by checking these requirements before you begin.

Getting a permit takes some time and money, but it's well worth the effort. Work done with a permit is checked by a building inspector, who will tell you if there are mistakes in the construction. Having your work checked ensures that you will not create structural weaknesses in your home. Work done without the required permits may make the house more difficult to sell. Many states now have real-estate disclosure laws that require you to notify a potential buyer that work was done on the house without a permit. This usually raises suspicions about the integrity of the work. The cost of a permit will usually be repaid quite nicely.

Codes regulate most aspects of building. There are different model codes in the United States; they include the Basic National Building Code, the Standard Building Code, and the Uniform Building Code. There are also local codes, which may differ from the model codes.

Model codes are published in books that can make interesting reading. Code books may be a bit expensive, and they can be difficult for a beginner to use, but they are packed with information. Some local building departments have very useful written information specifically designed to help the owner-builder to understand local building codes. Remember that it is easier to get it right the first time, and don't be afraid to ask questions.

Safety

Before you start cutting up lumber, think hard about safety. Always be careful to read all the instructions that come with your tools, particularly if you are relatively unfamiliar with power equipment. Don't try to use inferior tools. If the cost of professional tools seems forbidding, and if you don't expect to use them again, consider buying top-grade professional tools and then selling them to someone in the trades after you have finished the project. You should be able to sell good tools quite easily.

Always wear appropriate safety equipment. Use safety glasses or goggles. Don't forget to protect your ears. Many people do not realize that they can permanently damage their hearing by carelessly exposing themselves to construction-site noise. Very light and comfortable hearing protectors are available that resemble stereo headphones. They'll hang comfortably around your neck when you aren't using them. Be aware of dust hazards, especially when you are sawing or sanding. Paper masks are fine for most kinds of dust. Finally, wear a heavy-duty painter's mask with a carbon filter when you work with paint, solvent, or glue. Chemical products are clearly labeled, and masks are also labeled to indicate what types of hazards they are rated for.

Opening Up a Platform-Framed Wall

Before you cut into any wall, either interior or exterior, find out whether that wall is bearing or nonbearing. A bearing wall carries weight from above, such as a floor, a ceiling, or a roof load. A nonbearing wall acts only as a partition and has only to support its own weight. Bearing walls are usually perpendicular to the floor, ceiling, or roof framing; the ends of the joists or rafters rest on the top plate of the bearing wall and transfer their load to that wall. You can usually see the direction of the framing in the attic and in the basement or the crawl space.

It can sometimes be tricky to find out which way the floor joists are running in the second floor of a house, but it mostly just takes a little detective work. Usually, but not always, they run in the same direction as the first floor and the ceiling. You may find it useful to purchase an inexpensive electronic stud finder and use it to look for a 16-inch or 24-inch pattern of framing. The electronic stud finder is not to be confused with the older magnetic stud finders, which are more difficult to use. They work by finding the nails in the stud, as opposed to sensing the mass of the stud or joist itself. You can also find the joists by tapping or, if you don't mind patching the ceiling in question, by driving small finishing nails up through the wallboard. Locate

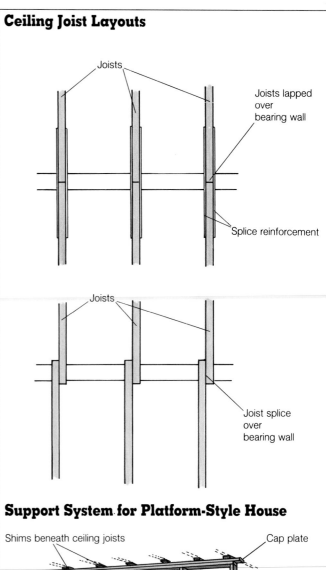

Ceiling Joist Layouts

Joists

Joists lapped over bearing wall

Splice reinforcement

Joists

Joist splice over bearing wall

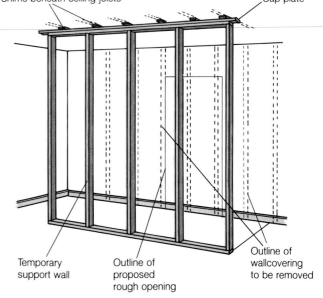

Support System for Platform-Style House

Shims beneath ceiling joists

Cap plate

Temporary support wall

Outline of proposed rough opening

Outline of wallcovering to be removed

Door Opening in Platform-Style House

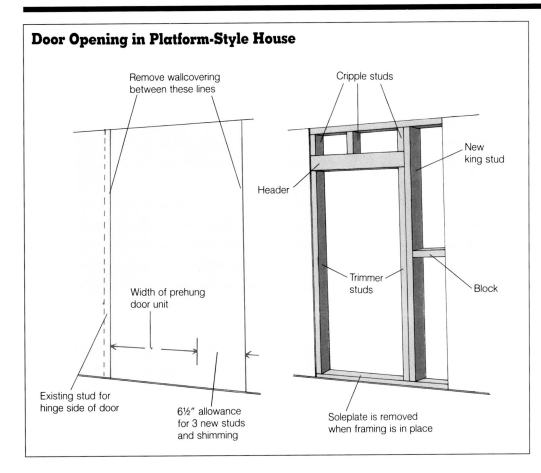

Remove wallcovering between these lines

Cripple studs

New king stud

Header

Width of prehung door unit

Trimmer studs

Block

Existing stud for hinge side of door

6½" allowance for 3 new studs and shimming

Soleplate is removed when framing is in place

at least three or four joists in a row that have the same spacing, to make sure that you aren't just hitting some miscellaneous blocking. Finally, be aware that sometimes hidden framing changes direction.

Watch out for special cases. For instance, although the gable end wall of a house is not generally perpendicular to the floor and roof framing, it may carry considerable weight of its own, particularly if it is large, with a heavy finish, such as stucco. Think carefully before you cut a big opening in such a wall. Some houses may have a ridge beam supported by posts in the gable end walls. The load of that ridge beam

must be supported if you make openings in the gable end wall below it.

When you are sure that you have located the bearing walls, set up temporary supports for any ceiling, floor, or roof that the wall in question supports. This section describes how to do the work in buildings that are platform framed. Balloon-framed construction is discussed on page 25.

To support a ceiling or floor above the wall in which you plan to cut an opening, construct a temporary stud wall 3 to 4 feet back from the existing wall. This will support the joists and still leave space for you to work. It is built just like a regular wall, with studs spaced on 16-inch centers,

a bottom plate, and a double top plate. Build the wall just short enough not to touch the ceiling. Then drive shims in from each side over the top plate at each floor joist. Rather than using what are commonly sold as shim shingles, splurge on one bundle of No. 1 sidewall shingles. They won't crush under a load, and their better quality makes them easier to work with.

Wires in the Walls

The wall where you want to make an opening is very likely to contain electrical wires. In older homes you may find what is known as knob-and-tube wiring. It derives its name

from the shape of the porcelain insulators used to attach the wiring to the framing. Usually these systems were installed with two insulated wires running parallel to each other a foot or so apart. However, they occasionally run singly, so don't assume that a lone wire is not hot. Newer houses use nonmetallic sheathed cable (NM, also known by the trade name Romex), which combines two insulated conductors, and usually a ground, in a thermoplastic sheathing. You may also run into wire in metal conduit or flexible armored cable. Altering NM systems is usually within the ability of the do-it-yourselfer. Generally, wire that goes across the opening you want to make will be rerouted by installing a new outlet on either side of the opening. The two outlets are then connected with a wire that goes over the top of the door opening, or down through the floor and the basement or crawl space, to reconnect the circuit. Non-NM wiring should be altered by an electrician, unless you have experience working with the system in question.

Pipes in the Walls

You may run across water, gas, or drain and vent lines in the walls, particularly if you are working on a two-story house. Water will be in galvanized steel, copper, or plastic pipes. Soldering copper is not difficult, nor is cutting and fitting plastic pipe. Galvanized steel is best left to a plumber.

Gas lines are run with plain steel pipe, although plumbers have been known to throw in galvanized pipe or fittings if that is more convenient than

Rerouting Electrical Cable and Plumbing Pipes

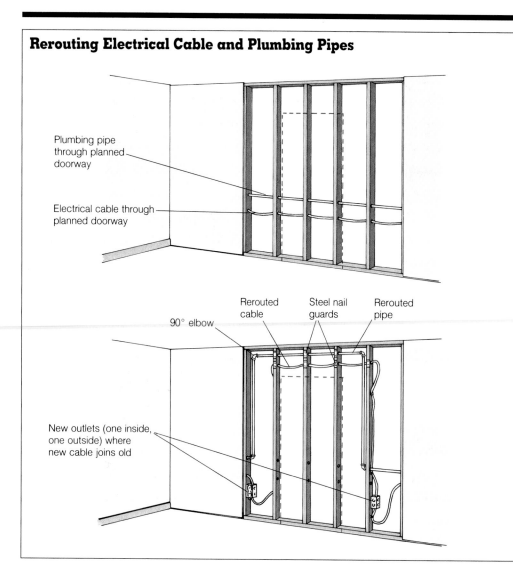

Plumbing pipe through planned doorway

Electrical cable through planned doorway

90° elbow

Rerouted cable

Steel nail guards

Rerouted pipe

New outlets (one inside, one outside) where new cable joins old

Always install a steel protector plate on the face of the member just in front of any wire or pipe that you move. This will prevent you from driving a wallboard nail or a trim nail through the wire or pipe later on.

Making the Opening

Start by removing the inside wallcovering on the wall in question. There are a couple of ways to do this. If the wall is not too large—for instance, if it is one wall of a small bedroom—it might be best to remove the wallboard from the entire wall. This might sound strange, but you can do a perfect patch-in joint at the ceiling and corners of a wall. Patching one area in the middle of a wall is more difficult and is justified only if the wall is too large to remove completely. Consider too that if you are opening up an uninsulated exterior wall, it may be a good idea to remove all the wallboard and install insulation while you are at it.

If you are taking the whole wall off, cut the joint in the corners and at the ceiling. Be sure to cut the paper reinforcing tape in the joint, so that you don't accidentally peel the face paper off the wallboard on the adjacent surfaces. If the wall is too big to remove all the wallboard, mark a vertical line from floor to ceiling a foot or two to the left and to the right of the new opening. It is necessary to remove enough wallcovering to accommodate the opening, plus a space extending over to the next stud on each side. The cut on each side should be centered over a stud. Remove the baseboard before you do any cutting.

driving back to town. Because installing gas lines is difficult and potentially dangerous, this job is best left to the plumber.

Drain and vent lines will be made of cast iron or ABS (acrylonitrile-butadiene-styrene) plastic. These lines range from 1½ inches to 4 inches in diameter. ABS is easy enough to work with, but you must be sure you understand the drainage and venting principles involved. Water flows through these pipes only by gravity, so it won't do to reroute a pipe over the top of the opening. Proper "fall" must be

maintained in the system. If you have a plumber working on other types of pipe, you can ask how to approach ABS modifications. Cast iron requires specialized equipment and is best left to the plumber.

If the heating system consists of a hot-water boiler and radiators, the pipes should be moved by a heating contractor. How the pipes are run can drastically affect the performance of the system. With forced-air heating there will be ducts in the walls. These are

fairly easy to move if you have a crawl space or a basement, and parts are readily available. You'll probably need a heating contractor if special parts must be fabricated.

Although all of the utility connections may be installed in the walls, it is highly unlikely that all of them will be in the wall you want to open up. In fact, unless you are in a bathroom, laundry, or kitchen, the odds are excellent that the only thing you will come across will be one electrical line, running horizontally 1 to 3 feet off the floor.

Making the Cut

There are two ways to do this. One is to set the depth of cut on a circular saw to slightly over the thickness of the wallcovering—say ⅝ inch for ½-inch wallboard. Use a carbide blade, since you will be going right through the wallboard nails in the stud under the cut. This method has the advantages of being fast and producing a clean edge. The disadvantage is that it will also produce a tremendous amount of dust. Be sure to wear safety glasses, a dust mask, and hearing protection. At each end, where the saw cannot reach, finish the cut with a very sharp utility knife. Also use a utility knife to cut the joint where the wall meets the ceiling.

The other way is to use a utility knife for the whole cut. This method is a bit slower, and you will have to pick your way around the nails in the stud (remove them as you go). The advantage is that you won't raise clouds of dust.

Now pull the wallboard out between the two cuts. If you can't get it started, take a hammer and carefully punch a hole big enough to get your hand into. Watch out for wires or pipes behind the spot where you are hitting. Once you can get your hand into the opening, you can pull off the wallboard in big chunks. You can also use a hammer or the curved end of a crowbar to help pull it away. If there is insulation in the wall, wear a dust mask, long pants, and a long-sleeved shirt while you remove it. Watch out for wires that may be hidden by the

insulation. At this point it is a good idea to turn off electricity to the area and to run lights and tools with an extension cord plugged into another circuit. However, you should still treat the wires as though they were hot. It's easy to make mistakes about circuits, especially in an older house that may have been rewired. If a wire must be moved, and you cannot be absolutely certain that you have turned its circuit off, the only safe procedure is to switch off all of the electricity in the house.

If you are working on an interior wall, use the same procedure to remove the wall covering on both sides. If you are working on an exterior wall, you probably will not have to cut away the siding until the new framing is complete.

The next step is to remove the old studs that are in the new opening. If they are 2 by 4s, you can cut almost across them with a circular saw; then you may be able to pry them toward you, breaking them and removing the pieces. Often, though, the siding is too firmly attached to the studs—or you may be dealing with 2 by 6 framing. In these cases, pry the siding away from the studs just enough to get the metal-cutting blade of a reciprocating saw behind them in order to snip the nails. If you can cut all the nails between the siding and the studs, you should be able to remove the studs by banging them sideways at the bottom with a sledgehammer or a hand sledge.

The next step is to install the first king stud. If you can be slightly flexible about the location of the new door, you can use one of the existing studs as the king stud. However, be sure that it is plumb. If it isn't, you may be able to bang it over to plumb with the sledgehammer. If the siding nails are holding it too tightly, you are better off installing a new king stud next to the old one, shimming as necessary to make it plumb. If you install a new king stud not nailed to the existing stud, cut a trimmer, nail it and the king together, and install them as a unit. If you are using the existing stud, nail the trimmer to the king. Facenail with 16d nails and toenail at the top and bottom with 8d nails.

It is common to find that the studs in the wall are of a different width than the studs you are installing. If this is the case, line up the outside face of the new studs flush with the outside face of the old studs. Then rip furring strips of the correct thickness to bring the inside face of the new framing in line with the existing framing.

You will need to know the rough-opening dimension of the door you are installing. If you are making the jamb, a trimmer length of 80 inches should work with a standard door. If you are using a prehung door package, look at the door or at the instructions to see how thick the sill of the unit is. Then decide how high the top of the sill should be in order to match the finish floor.

To frame a door in special situations—such as this one, with sidelights and a semicircular transom—it's best to seek the advice of an architect or a contractor.

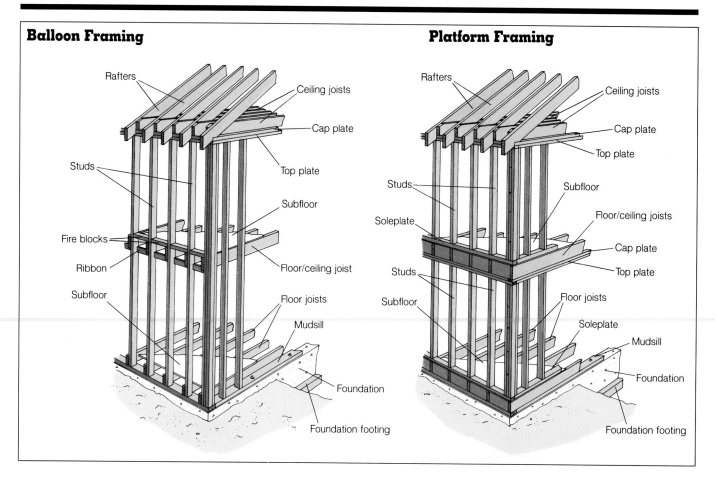

Balloon Framing

Rafters
Ceiling joists
Cap plate
Studs
Top plate
Subfloor
Fire blocks
Ribbon
Floor/ceiling joist
Subfloor
Floor joists
Mudsill
Foundation
Foundation footing

Platform Framing

Rafters
Ceiling joists
Cap plate
Top plate
Studs
Subfloor
Soleplate
Floor/ceiling joists
Cap plate
Studs
Top plate
Subfloor
Floor joists
Soleplate
Mudsill
Foundation
Foundation footing

There is no hard-and-fast rule about this, because there is so much possible variation in the thickness of the finish floor and the subfloor.

Try this: Determine how much of the subfloor, if any, needs to be cut away to get the sill of the door unit at the correct height to match the finish floor. Take that dimension, subtract it from the manufacturer's rough-opening height measurement, and then subtract 1½ inches to allow for the bottom plate. That should be the correct trimmer height. Note that you may not have to cut away any subfloor below the doorsill.

You should now have one king and trimmer installed.

Note the manufacturer's rough-opening width dimension, or in the case of a standard door, add 2½ inches for jambs and shimming, and make a mark on the bottom plate that distance over from the first king and trimmer. Mark the top plates also, keeping in mind that the trimmer does not extend to the top plate, so it is the king stud that you will be marking. Cut and install the second king and trimmer. Make sure that both kings and trimmers are plumb. Measure across the top, between the two kings, to find the length of the header. Cut and install the header and fill in the space over it with cripple studs.

Shrinkage in the header sometimes causes settlement cracks around doors and

windows. If you are concerned about shrinkage, consider using kiln-dried lumber around the new opening, particularly for the header.

Existing openings can be altered using many of the principles outlined above. If the new opening will be smaller than the existing one, simply cut new studs to reduce the size of the latter. If the new opening will be larger than the existing one, the old header and framing must be pulled out and replaced.

Once the old framing is removed or altered, cut away the siding, and also the bottom plate where it crosses the opening. The siding will be easier to cut if you first make sure that it is nailed to the edges of the

new opening. Use a circular saw or a reciprocating saw. The sill is best removed with a reciprocating saw.

Again, you may have to cut away some of the flooring or subflooring to get the doorsill at the correct height. This height will vary depending on the door and on the finish floor. With traditional doors a wood sill is meant to sit at such a height that the back edge is flush with the finish floor. The joint is then covered with another piece, called the threshold. How the floor will be cut away depends on the construction of the house. The important thing is that the joint between the sill and the floor must be fully supported. You may have to add blocking to accomplish this.

Balloon Framing

Balloon construction is different from platform construction, and it is shored up differently for structural changes. The studs in a balloon-framed building run the full height of the wall without interruption (see illustration at left). The floors are held up by a ribbon board let into the studs, and the floor joists are nailed to the sides of the studs. Shoring is still necessary to hold up the ceiling joists and floor joists, but because the roof load in balloon framing comes all the way down the wall, without being supported by the second floor, there must also be a way to hold up the wall studs.

Prepare the wall by removing the wallcovering as described on pages 22 to 23. Then tack a 2 by 8 waler (a temporary horizontal brace) across the top of the studs. Drill holes through the waler into the studs and attach it with ⅜-inch by 5-inch lag screws. For extra support cut a 2 by 4 brace to fit under each end of the waler. You can now safely remove the studs in the opening and proceed to frame it as described for platform construction.

Support System for Balloon-Style House

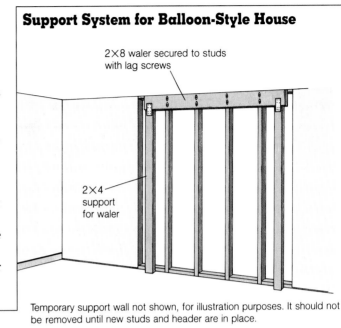

2×8 waler secured to studs with lag screws

2×4 support for waler

Temporary support wall not shown, for illustration purposes. It should not be removed until new studs and header are in place.

Door Opening in Balloon-Style House

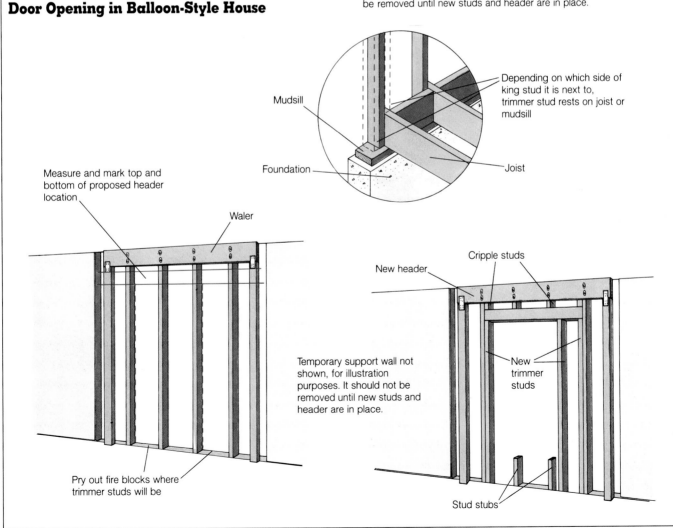

Mudsill

Foundation

Depending on which side of king stud it is next to, trimmer stud rests on joist or mudsill

Joist

Measure and mark top and bottom of proposed header location

Waler

Pry out fire blocks where trimmer studs will be

Cripple studs

New header

New trimmer studs

Temporary support wall not shown, for illustration purposes. It should not be removed until new studs and header are in place.

Stud stubs

INSTALLING THE DOOR

Once the rough framing is done, you can start on the real fun of installing the door. Be sure to read any instructions that come with it before you begin installation.

Installing a Prehung Door

Prehung doors are available with or without trim (see page 12). To illustrate a typical installation, this section uses the common example of a prehung unit with wood trim. These units are installed by nailing right through the face of the trim into the siding and framing around the rough opening.

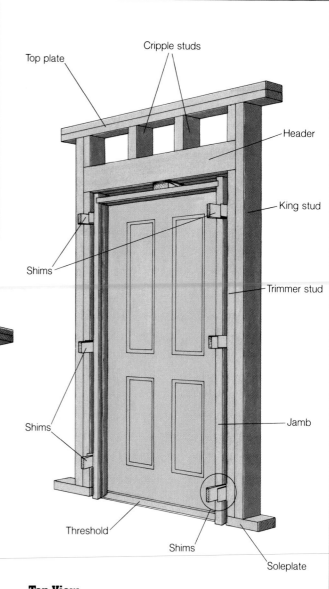

Top plate • Cripple studs • Header • King stud • Trimmer stud • Shims • Jamb • Shims • Threshold • Shims • Soleplate

Installing a Prehung Door

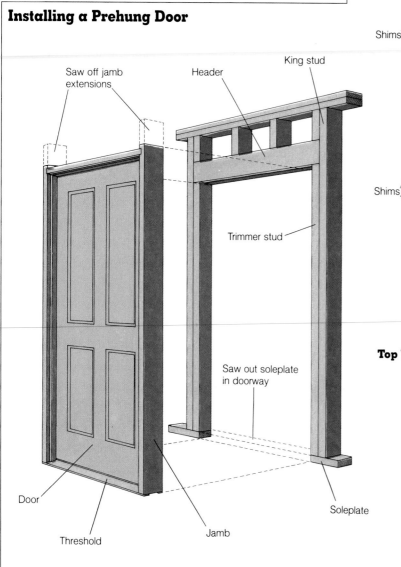

Saw off jamb extensions • Header • King stud • Trimmer stud • Saw out soleplate in doorway • Soleplate • Door • Threshold • Jamb

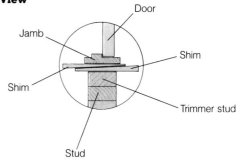

Top View

Door • Jamb • Shim • Shim • Stud • Trimmer stud

Before you start moving the door, a word of caution: You may have got used to wearing a tool belt while you did the rough framing. Be careful not to get the tool belt between yourself and the door that you are carrying. You'll scratch the glass or mar the finish if you do.

In some cases, you will need to install a strip of felt around the door opening before you hang the door. See the section on weatherproofing (pages 34 and 35).

If the unit is too large and heavy for you to move safely, remove the hinge pins and take the doors out of their jamb. Temporarily tack the jamb in place in the opening. Then re-install the doors and the hinge pins. Make sure that the door unit can't be knocked over by a bump or a gust of wind; brace it securely.

Now shim and adjust the door unit so that it is square and opens and closes smoothly. As you look at the door in its opening, pay attention to the small space between the door itself and the jamb. You'll notice that as the top of the door unit is leaned to the right or the left, this small space will either open up or close up in different spots. Ideally, if the door is perfectly square, the space should be even all the way around. If there isn't enough space in one spot, that's where the door will bind.

Notice the spaces above and below the door. If they are not even all the way across, the subfloor may not be level under the door. Planing or shimming may be needed. In some cases, the structure beneath the floor may need repairs. These repairs can be complicated

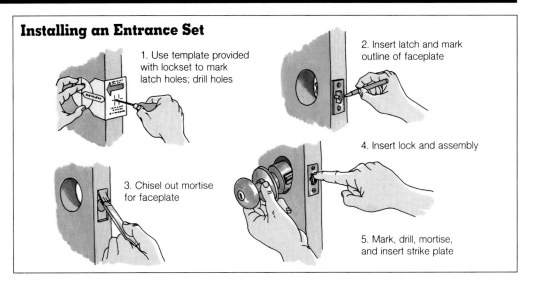

Installing an Entrance Set

1. Use template provided with lockset to mark latch holes; drill holes

2. Insert latch and mark outline of faceplate

3. Chisel out mortise for faceplate

4. Insert lock and assembly

5. Mark, drill, mortise, and insert strike plate

and expensive, so seek expert advice if you discover a crooked floor.

Once the floor is level, tack the trim lightly (leaving the nailheads exposed in case they need to be removed) to the wall near the top of the jamb on the hinge side of the door and then to the jamb on the strike side of the door. Adjust the space around the door by sliding the bottom of the door unit left or right. If it's hard to move, a small crowbar between the rough framing and the jamb will give you plenty of leverage. Once the spacing looks good, open and close the door a few times to make sure that it is operating smoothly. When you are certain that the door fits the opening properly, either remove the unit or have a helper lean it outward so that you can caulk around the opening, beneath where the trim will be. Reinstall and readjust the door, again just tacking it in place. One of the commonest mistakes beginners make is to pound all of the nails home

when installing a door. Leave them with their heads sticking out until you are absolutely sure that the door is properly adjusted. This will make it much easier to remove the nails if necessary.

It's common for one or more of the jambs to have enough of a bow that the space between the door and the jamb will vary, no matter how you adjust the door from side to side. Adjust the door as well as you can and then work your way down each jamb, shimming it in or out to correct the space as you nail the trim to the wall. Don't drive the nails in yet. When the jambs are fully adjusted and the door operates smoothly, you can drive the nails home.

Attach the trim with hot-dipped galvanized nails. Countersink the nail heads with a nail hammer and a nail set; then fill the holes with putty, sand until smooth, and paint the trim. If the door is already painted a color you like, and you want to avoid having to fill the nail holes, use stainless steel ring-shank finishing nails, which are available in many lumberyards. They are expensive, but it takes only a few

to install a door. Since they will not rust and cause streaks, you need not countersink them. The heads themselves are fairly small, and the nails often come ready-painted, so you might not even need to touch them up.

Now finish attaching the jambs to the framing. Read the manufacturer's instructions carefully. As a rule, the jambs are shimmed and then nailed through the shims into the framing, particularly at stress points such as the strike and the hinges. However, because designs differ, it is important to follow the manufacturer's instructions on this point precisely. The sill itself is usually screwed to the floor.

The space between the jamb and the framing must be sealed to stop drafts. One product that can be used for this purpose is a foam that is applied from a pressurized can. It expands to fill the gap and then hardens quickly. Be very careful with this product if you use it. The foam expands so vigorously that if you use too much, it will actually push out the jambs

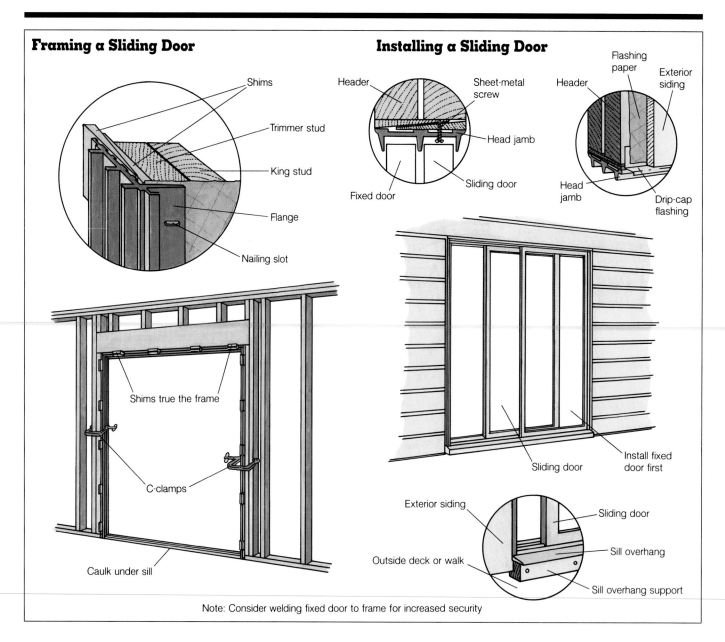

Framing a Sliding Door

Shims

Trimmer stud

King stud

Flange

Nailing slot

Shims true the frame

C-clamps

Caulk under sill

Installing a Sliding Door

Header

Sheet-metal screw

Head jamb

Fixed door

Sliding door

Header

Flashing paper

Exterior siding

Head jamb

Drip-cap flashing

Sliding door

Install fixed door first

Exterior siding

Sliding door

Sill overhang

Outside deck or walk

Sill overhang support

Note: Consider welding fixed door to frame for increased security

---

and ruin the fine fit you worked so hard to achieve. Be sparing until you get a feel for the right amount. Various solid-foam tubes or rods are also available; these can be stuffed into the space.

Installing a Metal Sliding Door

Metal sliding doors are installed in much the same way as hinged doors. One difference is that instead of nailing the unit in through a finished wood trim, you will be nailing through a metal fin that runs all the way around the door. This fin is covered later with trim or siding. Again, do not drive any nails home until the unit is adjusted and the doors slide freely.

Metal- and vinyl-clad doorframes are a sort of hybrid. They most closely resemble metal-framed doors. The cladding itself may include a nailing fin, or there may be a nailing fin that is attached on-site to the door—usually a simple operation. Again, the fin is covered with trim or siding.

Try to have the doors delivered and on hand at the time you do the rough framing. If this isn't possible, be sure you get a copy of the installation instructions for your particular doors so you're sure the rough opening is the correct size. The rough opening should be whatever size the manufacturer specifies, usually ½ inch wider and ½ inch taller than the door unit.

Take special care to make sure the trimmer studs are plumb and the header is level. Minor variations can be corrected with shims, but it's a lot easier if they're perfectly true to start with.

Hanging Your Own Door

To achieve a more custom-made appearance, you can hang your own door. As a rule, you would go to this much trouble only for an exterior door; prehung units are usually adequate for interior installations. This section explains how to hang an exterior door; an interior door is hung in the same way, except that the sill and the threshold are not needed. Exterior doors of homes always open inward, with the handle on the same side as the light switch.

To hang your own door, you will need the door itself, three butt hinges, sill material, a threshold, a door handle and a dead bolt, side and head jambs, doorstops, exterior and interior trim, and weather stripping.

Installing a Doorjamb

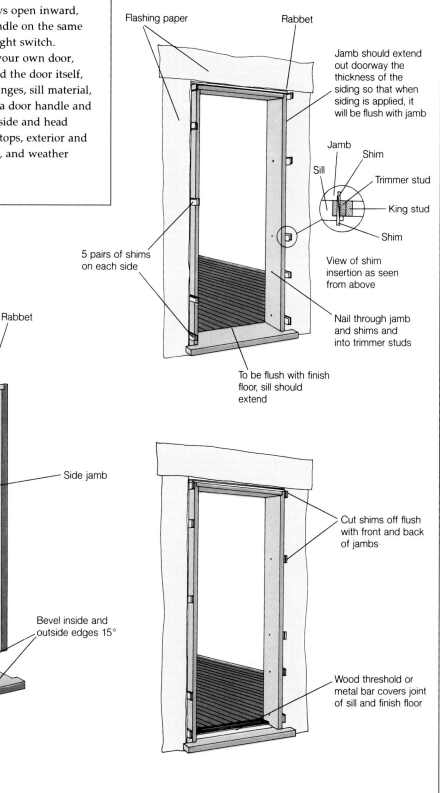

Rabbet

Rabbet

Head jamb

Side jamb

Side jamb

15°

Bevel inside and outside edges 15°

Sill

Drip groove

Frame Installation

Flashing paper

Rabbet

Jamb should extend out doorway the thickness of the siding so that when siding is applied, it will be flush with jamb

Jamb

Shim

Sill

Trimmer stud

King stud

Shim

View of shim insertion as seen from above

5 pairs of shims on each side

Nail through jamb and shims and into trimmer studs

To be flush with finish floor, sill should extend

Cut shims off flush with front and back of jambs

Wood threshold or metal bar covers joint of sill and finish floor

Installing Doorsills

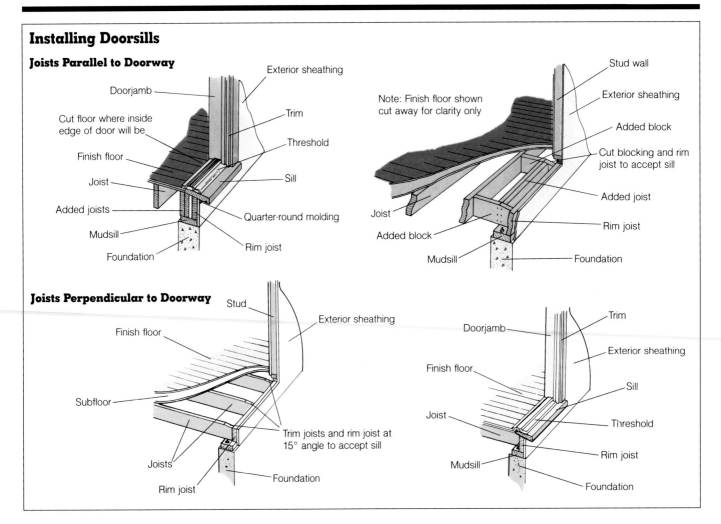

Joists Parallel to Doorway

- Doorjamb
- Cut floor where inside edge of door will be
- Finish floor
- Joist
- Added joists
- Mudsill
- Foundation
- Exterior sheathing
- Trim
- Threshold
- Sill
- Quarter-round molding
- Rim joist

Note: Finish floor shown cut away for clarity only

- Stud wall
- Exterior sheathing
- Added block
- Cut blocking and rim joist to accept sill
- Added joist
- Rim joist
- Foundation
- Joist
- Added block
- Mudsill

Joists Perpendicular to Doorway

- Stud
- Finish floor
- Subfloor
- Joists
- Rim joist
- Exterior sheathing
- Trim joists and rim joist at 15° angle to accept sill
- Foundation

- Doorjamb
- Finish floor
- Joist
- Mudsill
- Trim
- Exterior sheathing
- Sill
- Threshold
- Rim joist
- Foundation

Installing the Sill

In new construction, or when you cut a new opening, you must install a doorsill. It provides a finished appearance, and its downward slope sheds water that blows against the house.

Sills are sold at lumberyards and home-improvement centers. They are made of hardwood and should have a groove on the underside near the front to prevent water from running along the bottom edge toward the house. If it doesn't have one, cut a ¼-inch-deep groove with a circular saw.

In new construction the floor joists must be trimmed to accept the sill so that its back edge is flush with the finish floor. The threshold will cover the joint between the floor and sill. When adding a new doorway to an existing house, you must cut the flooring and subflooring to expose the joists. Make the cut directly under the inside edge of the closed door.

If the joists run parallel to the sill, you must add a support member for the edge of the subflooring that was cut away and for the back of the sill. Do this by nailing two blocks, of the same dimension as the joists, between the joists on either side of the door opening. Cut two support joists to length and nail them through the blocks, as illustrated. One supports the flooring and the other supports the inner edge of the sill. Use a saw and chisel to notch the tops of the joists at the edge of the house. Make the notches 2 inches deep, fit the sill into this trimmed area, and check that it is level. Shim one

end if necessary. Predrill the nail holes. When the sill is nailed in place, apply a bead of caulk under the sill where it meets the siding. Then cover the joint with a length of quarter-round molding.

Installing the Jambs

It is easiest to buy material that is intended for doorjambs; it will already be routed for the head jamb and cut to size. If you make your own, use stock that is at least a full 1 inch thick and rip it to the width of the house framing material plus the thicknesses of the exterior and interior sidings. At the top of the side jambs, rout a ½-inch-deep rabbet the same thickness as the jamb material, so that the head jamb fits flush with the tops of the side jambs.

The rough door opening should be as wide as the door, plus the thickness of both side jambs, plus ½ inch on each side for shimming.

Put the jambs together with glue and three 8d casing nails in each side.

Install the shims in the opening, with two shims behind each hinge location and one or two more equally spaced between. Check that the frame is plumb and square. Then tack the top of the hinge side jamb in place.

Adjust the width of the jambs at the bottom to match the width at the top by tightening or loosening a drywall screw driven through the jamb into the trimmer stud. Check again that the jamb is square by placing a steel framing square in the corners. Check that the head jamb is level; if it isn't, shim the bottom of one leg.

When everything is square, double-check that the door closes evenly. Nail the jambs to the trimmer studs through the shims. Use 12d casing nails, with two at the top, two at the bottom, and six more evenly spaced between.

Trimming the Door

The door should be trimmed to ¼ inch less than the width of the jamb to give a ⅛-inch clearance on each side. In addition, trim the door to allow for weather stripping (see page 35). Do all the trimming for width on the hinge stile so you won't have to deepen the lock mortise.

The last step is to bevel the inner edge of the lock stile ⅛ inch with a jack plane so it will clear the weather stripping as it closes.

Allow ⅛ inch of clearance at the top and bottom. The door will be cut to fit the threshold and the weather stripping after it is hung.

Installing the Hinges

On doors up to 7 feet high, use three 4-inch butt hinges (or decorative hinges). On doors over 7 feet high, use four hinges. The door and the jamb must be mortised so the hinges will be flush with the surface. Set the door on edge and brace it in the corner of a room, or use one of the door bucks shown in the illustration on page 33.

Exact hinge locations vary according to taste, but one common practice is to place the top of the highest hinge 7 inches from the top of the door and the bottom of the lowest hinge 11 inches from the bottom of the door. Space the other hinge evenly between the first two.

Suggested Door Hinge Sizes

For appearance's sake as well as utility, be sure your doors are on hinges appropriate for their width, thickness, and use.

Door Thickness (In.)	Door Width (In.)	Hinge Size (In.)
¾–1⅛ (cabinets)	Up to 24	2½
⅞–1⅛ (screen or storm)	Up to 36	3
1⅜ (passage)	Up to 32	3½
	Over 32	4
1¾ (passage or entry)	Up to 36	4½
	Over 36	5
2 (entry)	Up to 42	5 or 6

Trace the outline of the hinge on the edge of the stile with a sharp pencil or a knife. Allow the leaf to extend ¼ inch beyond the edge, so that the knuckle will not bind against the casing when the door is fully open. Remember that the knuckle is inside, not outside, the house.

After the mortises are cut (see page 32), put the hinges in place and mark the center of each screw hole. Punch each mark with a nail before drilling to ensure that the drill bit does not slip off center. Be sure to drill straight holes; if the screw goes in crooked, it will pull the hinge out of alignment.

With the door hinges installed, put the door in the jamb and mark the hinge locations, keeping the face of the door flush with the jamb. This is easier said than done, so

arrange to have a helper. Put small shims under the door to raise it to ⅛ inch below the top. Mark the tops and bottoms of the hinges with a sharp pencil or a knife. Remove the door and trace hinge outlines onto the jamb where you made the marks. Then cut the mortises in the jamb just as you did in the door.

A good trick is to mark and cut the top hinge first. Put the door up, screw the top hinge to the jamb, and then check the other marks and make adjustments before you cut them.

If you attach the halves of a hinge separately and they do not line up when you put the door in place, loosen the screws on both leaves. While a helper supports the door, tap the leaves together. Insert the pin and tighten the screws.

When the door is up, check that it closes without binding anywhere. Ideally, there will be a ⅛-inch clearance on each side. For the perfect door, take it down and trim for ³⁄₁₆ inch of clearance on the lock stile, using a sharp jack plane.

Cutting Mortises

Hinge mortises can be cut with a router and a commercially available hinge mortise template, a hinge marker, or the tried-and-true hammer and chisel. Except with the template, the outline and depth of the mortise must be marked on the wood with a sharp pencil, awl, or knife.

When using a router and template, carefully read the instructions that come with the template; be sure you understand them. You will need a straight routing bit and a guide bushing for the router. With wing nuts or knobs, clamp the template to the edge of the door. Adjust the router bit to the depth of the hinge thickness. Set the router in place and squeeze the trigger.

If the hinges have square corners, square the corners of

Cutting for Hinges

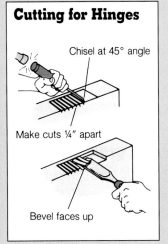

Chisel at 45° angle

Make cuts ¼" apart

Bevel faces up

Routing for Hinges

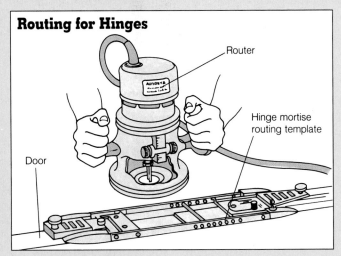

Router

Hinge mortise routing template

Door

the mortise with a chisel. However, you can buy hinges with round corners designed to fit into router-cut mortises.

To cut mortises by hand, use a ½- or ¾-inch chisel. Score the top and bottom edges of the mortise by

hammering the chisel, with the bevel inward, to the depth of the mortise. Between the scores make a series of similar cuts about ¼ inch apart. Then score the back line of the mortise in the same way as you scored the top and bottom lines.

Remove the waste wood in the mortise by driving the chisel from the edge toward the back line at the depth line; the bevel of the chisel should face up. Set the hinge in the mortise to check the fit. Make any final adjustments, and clean up the corners.

Doorstops

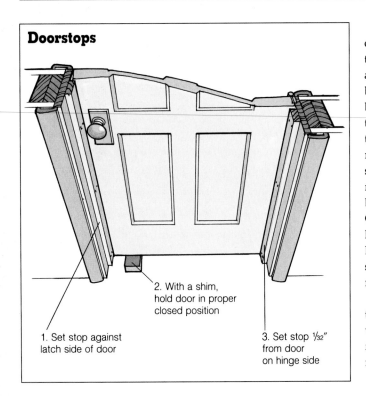

1. Set stop against latch side of door

2. With a shim, hold door in proper closed position

3. Set stop ¹⁄₃₂" from door on hinge side

If the door sticks at the top of the jamb and the gap between door and jamb is wider at the bottom, the problem may be a jamb that is not plumb, a bottom-hinge mortise that is too deep, or a top-hinge mortise that is too shallow. To correct the first two problems, shim the bottom hinge. To make a shim, use the cardboard box that the hinges came in. Cut a strip the height of the hinge and about ¼ inch wide. Loosen the hinge on the jamb, slip the shim behind it, and retighten the screws.

If the door is binding at the top because the top mortise wasn't cut deeply enough, remove the door and chisel the mortise deeper.

Installing the Stops

Last of all, install the doorstops. These are made of ½-inch by 1½-inch material. While you hold the door closed at the proper position, have a helper trace the outside edge of the door along the jamb with a sharp pencil. Measure and cut the stops to length. First, nail on the head stop along the line; then nail on the two legs. For greater security, stops for exterior doors can be milled as an integral part of the jamb so that they cannot be pried off.

Using Door Bucks

A door buck allows you to stand a door on edge while you plane it or mortise the hinges. Door bucks are easy to make and will save you a lot of time and frustration. This section describes two door bucks you can make with scrap lumber in a few minutes. Make them both and see which you find easiest to use.

To make the first buck, cut a couple of pieces of ⅜- or ¼-inch plywood 3½ inches wide and 12 inches long. Nail 2 pieces of 2 by 4, about 4 inches long, on edge near the center of each. Space them apart the thickness of a door plus ⅛ inch. Then nail square 2 by 4 legs at the ends, and you are ready to work. Just set the door on the buck and the weight will bend the strip of plywood down, clamping the door between the two 2 by 4s.

Make the second buck from lengths of 2 by 4 about 16 inches long. Cut a notch 1 inch deep and 2½ inches wide in the center of the 2 by 4s. From a scrap of 1 by 3 or 1 by 4, cut a wedge about 5 inches long (see the illustration). Set the door in the notch, and knock the wedge in to hold the door upright.

Another simple and very sturdy door buck is probably already in your arsenal of tools: a supply of pipe or bar clamps. Using clamps is a little more cumbersome and takes longer than using a real door buck, but if you have only a few doors to work on, clamps work fine. Just place one near each end of the door—the bars or pipes should extend in opposite directions. To protect the door, put pieces of scrap wood in the jaws of the clamp.

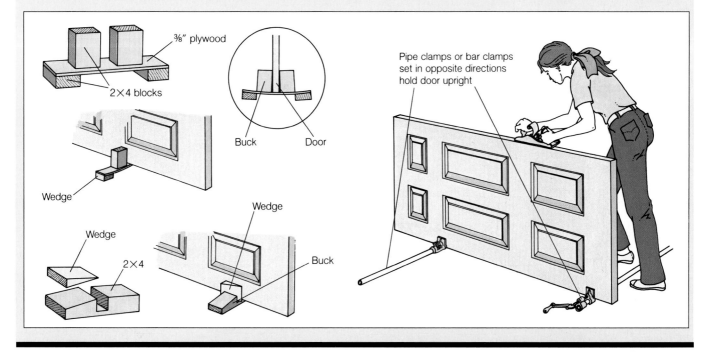

⅜" plywood

2×4 blocks

Buck   Door

Wedge

Wedge

Wedge

2×4

Buck

Pipe clamps or bar clamps set in opposite directions hold door upright

Installing the Threshold

After the sill is installed and the door is hung, remove the door again and install the threshold. If it is made of hardwood, drill holes and nail; if it is aluminum, use screws through the predrilled holes. Remember that the threshold must cover the gap between the sloping sill and the finish floor.

Measure the thickness of the threshold plus the weather stripping on the threshold, if any. Remove that amount of material from the bottom of the door. Check the installation instructions for the weather stripping to see if they call for a bevel cut (so that the door edge will ride over the stripping). If they do, set the saw angle before you make the cut. Use a circular saw with a fine-toothed blade, such as is used for cutting plywood. For a straight cut use a fence made by clamping a straight-edged board to the door to guide the saw. Place pieces of scrap wood between the clamps and your work to protect the door.

Finishing Touches

Finish the installation by adding the trim (see page 36). You may want to paint the door, but you can also show off fine wood grain by applying stain and a clear finish. A double coat of oil-based sanding sealer will ensure a handsome appearance.

It would be difficult to describe exactly how to weatherproof every known combination of door, siding, and trim. However, the principles are the same in every case. The following discussion of these principles provides all the information you will need to weatherproof your own particular door.

Flashing and Flashing Paper

These materials are commonly used in weatherproofing. Flashing is usually made of sheet metal; its purpose is to keep water out of the joints in the building. Flashing paper is used for the same general purpose. It is impregnated with tar to make it water-resistant. Metal flashing can be exposed to weather, but flashing paper must be covered. Some builders prefer to use felt paper, also called building felt, instead of flashing paper. The common weights of felt paper used around door installations are 15 and 30 pound. These products are available in a number of different grades designed for specific installations.

Traditionally, it was the flashing paper or felt paper that formed the final line of defense in weatherproofing a building. Caulks were much less reliable years ago than now, and it is still considered a good practice to rely on a well-papered siding job, rather than on caulk, to keep water out. The most basic illustration of how these papers work is provided by a plain wall with no openings. The paper is installed horizontally, starting at the bottom, typically in courses 3 feet wide. Each successive course overlaps the one below it, like fish scales. If water should find its way through an opening in the siding, it will not be able to get through the paper because of the way the paper is overlapped. That is simple enough. The hard part is maintaining the water barrier when the new door opening is installed.

Metal, plastic, and clad wood doors are installed by nailing through the nailing fin. On clad wood doors the fin is made of the same material as

Weatherproofing Exterior Doors

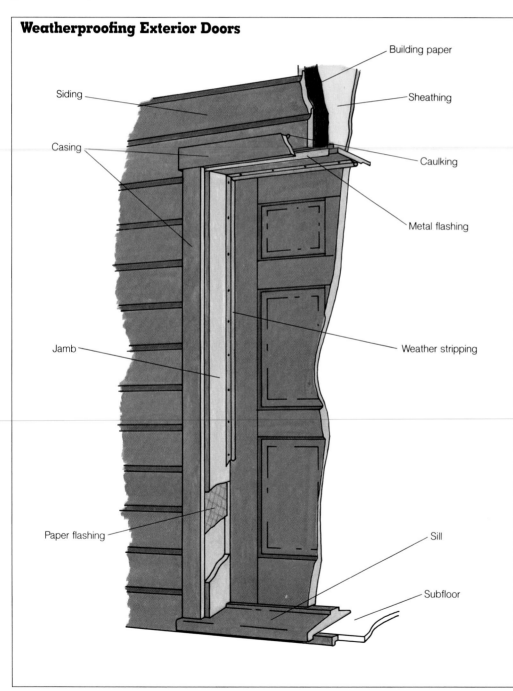

- Siding
- Casing
- Jamb
- Paper flashing
- Building paper
- Sheathing
- Caulking
- Metal flashing
- Weather stripping
- Sill
- Subfloor

the cladding. This fin also doubles as a sort of flashing for the head of the door. The paper above the door should overlap the fin, so that water cannot get under it. The trim is nailed over the fin to cover it. If the wall is going to be stuccoed, shingled, or sided, you could add a Z flashing over the trim piece at this point. It will be covered by the exterior siding. Plywood siding is a special case. Doors with fins are best installed before the plywood, which is then cut to fit around them. Gaps are caulked and are further protected by installing wood trim to cover the joint between the door and the plywood. Many types of plywood siding are rated for use without paper under them. It is not a bad idea to use the paper anyway, but don't be shocked if you find none under the existing plywood siding.

The sides and bottom of the doors need some attention too. Strips of flashing paper or 15-pound felt paper should be tacked around the rough opening before the door is hung. First, install a strip across the bottom of the door opening. You can use staples or roofing nails. This bottom strip should overlap the existing paper below it. Then install strips on the sides, overlapping the bottom strip. The strips on the sides of the opening should run up under the paper above the opening. It can be tricky to cut the wide felt paper that's already on the house to fit exactly over the narrow fin at the top of the door. It's easier if you first cut a narrow strip of felt

paper or use a length of flashing paper for the top. It should overlap the side strips and the nailing fin. Then when you notch the wide felt paper that's already on the house, it will overlap the top strip. Just keep thinking of fish scales.

Sometimes you may want to install a door that has nail-on wood trim right over existing siding. In this case, there will be nothing to hide a Z flashing if you use one. You can install a door over the siding using caulk with no felt or flashing, particularly if it's in a sheltered location, but this is not recommended. For a truly trouble-free installation, you'll have to come up with a creative way to get a Z flashing in. Old-timers used to make a Z flashing out of lead, which was carefully formed over the top of the trim and then nailed at tiny intervals with small nails, tight to the siding. The joint was puttied and the Z flashing was painted to match the trim. Another solution is to fabricate a Z flashing with a small return that tucks into a shallow groove in the siding, which is then caulked. The groove can be made very easily with a circular saw. Set the blade at an appropriate depth and tack a straight piece of wood across the door trim to serve as a guide. Use a chisel to finish the ends.

You may find that there is no felt or flashing paper under your siding, but rather a white, paperlike membrane. This is one of the modern housewraps, spun from synthetic fibers. Treat them in the same way as paper. When working with nailing fins, be particularly

sure that the top fin is under the housewrap, and that the side and bottom fins are over it. This may take a little cutting at the top corners of the housewrap. You can repair the cuts with a little caulk.

Caulking Materials

There is a bewildering array of caulks from which to choose. Generally speaking, it is not a good idea to try to save money on caulk, when the potential cost of water damage is so high. You want to use the caulks that the best builders use. Look for them in professional lumberyards. Two good sources for heavy-duty caulks are marine suppliers and companies that manufacture and install skylights and greenhouses.

Some of the toughest and most reliable caulks are polyurethane formulations. These are designed for demanding applications, such as sealing high-rise exteriors. Use polyurethane in situations where the bead will be exposed to sun and weather. Silicone is often touted as an indestructible caulk. The caulk itself may be indestructible, but it has a bad tendency to let go of porous materials, such as wood. It adheres tenaciously to glass, metal, and tile—hence its usefulness in bathrooms—but for exposed beads, such as those around wood trim, polyurethane is far superior. An old reliable formulation is butyl caulk, readily available almost

anywhere. Butyl has decent durability, particularly if it is being used in a situation where it will be covered by a nailing fin or by trim. It also sticks very well. It is stringy and messy to work with, however. Your last choice is a latex caulk, or acrylic latex with silicone added. These perform decently in covered situations, but they are not durable enough for harsh exposures.

Weather Stripping

If you are installing a ready-made door unit, it will include weather stripping, but if you are hanging your own exterior door, you'll have to weather-strip it yourself.

Various types of weather stripping are sold at lumberyards and home-improvement centers. Some are designed to be installed on existing doors. The better types actually fit into slots in the jambs, which makes them less noticeable, but the door must be trimmed to take them. Thus, if you are hanging your own door, it is wise to choose the weather stripping first, so that you can accommodate it right from the start, rather than having to modify the door or the jamb later. Door sweeps seal out drafts at the bottom of the door. The best ones are adjustable, so that you can get them to seal snugly without binding up the operation of the door. Some sweeps are spring-loaded to rise up slightly when the door is open, thus providing more clearance for thick rugs, and to close snugly when the door is shut.

TRIMMING OUT THE DOOR

The functional job of trim is to cover the gap between the doorjamb and the siding. It is also used to attach the frames of some modern doors. In addition, the trim conveys a style, and it can be used to change the look of the door.

Corner Techniques

Lock-Nailed Joint

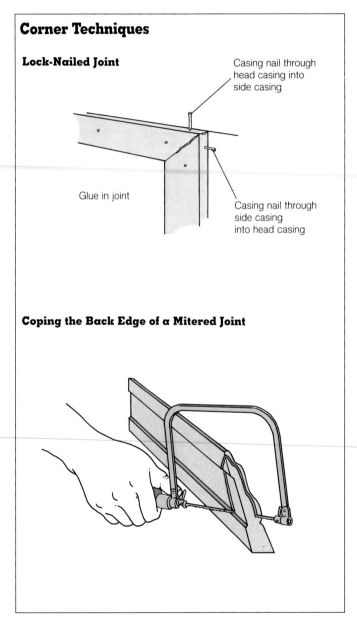

Casing nail through head casing into side casing

Glue in joint

Casing nail through side casing into head casing

Coping the Back Edge of a Mitered Joint

Kinds of Trim

If the doors are hung from their exterior trim, you need only fill the nail holes and paint. Traditional doors and clad units with nailing fins will both need to be trimmed out.

Start by trying to match the trim on the house. This is particularly easy to do if the trim is simple—perhaps no more complicated than a rectangular piece with a router pattern on the edges. Don't despair, though, if the trim you'd like to match is very ornate. Having custom trim matched and milled isn't cheap, but it is less expensive than most people think. There's probably a shop in your area that can do it. A large part of the cost is in setup, so be sure not to underestimate the amount of material you will need.

Assembling With Mitered Joints

The typical installation is done with mitered cuts at the corners. Ideally, the casing should be set back from the inner edges of the jamb by at least 3/16 inch and not more than 1/4 inch. Put a guideline on the side jamb to mark where the edge of the casing should be. To do this, adjust a combination square so that 3/16 inch protrudes and then slide the square along the jamb with a pencil tip following the edge of the blade. Mark the head jamb in the same way.

Once the jambs are marked, cut the base of one side casing at a 90-degree angle. Place the casing along the guideline on

the side jamb, then mark the top of the casing at the point where the lines on the side jamb and the head jamb meet. From that point make a 45-degree angle cut on the casing. Use a miter and a backsaw or a power miter saw. The work must be precise.

Nail the side casing in place. Then make a 45-degree cut on one end of the head casing and fit it to the side casing. Mark the other end at the point where the guidelines on the side and head jambs meet. From that point cut the head casing at a 45-degree angle. Nail up the head casing.

Finally, cut the bottom end of the other side casing at a 90-degree angle and put it in place. Mark where it meets the head casing, cut it, and nail it.

An Alternate Method

The foregoing description gives the textbook method of putting up trim where the door is square. Unfortunately, they often aren't. As a result the 45-degree cuts will not match up. Some pros do the job in the following way.

Mark the edges of the jambs 3/16 inch back, as described above. Cut the bottoms of the two side casings square and fit them against the side jambs. Note where the top ends meet the right angle of the guidelines on the head jamb. Mark the side casings at these two points. Cut a 45-degree angle in each one. Nail the side casings in place.

Interior Door Casings

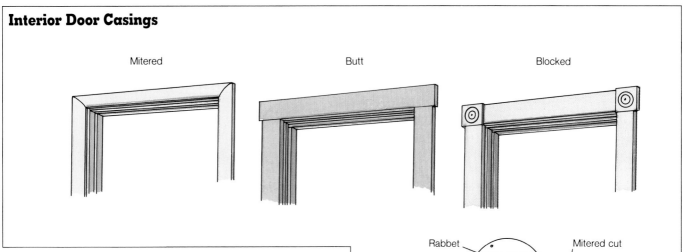

Mitered   Butt   Blocked

Next, take a length of trim for the head casing that is 4 inches longer on each side than the outer edges of the side casings. Cut 45-degree angles at both ends of the head casing. Now fit the left end of the head casing to the left side casing and position it precisely on the guideline. Let the other end overlap the casing on the other side. Check how the joint fits. If there is a gap, and all three casings are positioned exactly on the guidelines, then that side of the door is out of square. Check the joint on the other side in the same manner. If one side fits, put it in place. Then mark the top and bottom edges of the head casing to match the mitered cut on the other side casing. Adjust the miter saw to correspond and cut—but (an important "but") cut the head casing 1/16 inch longer than the space into which it will fit. Wedge it into position and nail. This helps to ensure a tight fit. If a small gap still exists, it can be tightened by lock nailing.

Assembling With Butt Joints

Installing casings with butt joints simplifies the job, and the result is still handsome. To achieve a varied effect, use a molded piece for the side and a solid piece for the head. The trim can also be made more attractive by using a head casing larger than the side casing. For example, if you use 1 by 3 stock for the side casing, use a 2 by 6 for the head casing. Use a router or a wood rasp to round off the outer edges of the head casing for a more finished appearance. You can also let the ends of the head casing extend beyond the sides by ½ inch to 1½ inches.

Before cutting the tops of the side casings, check that the head jamb is level. If it slopes slightly, adjust the cuts at the tops of the side casings. Use a long level to mark the cuts, cut the head casing, put it in place, and nail.

Corner Techniques

Professional-looking corners enhance the trim job. Two simple techniques can be used to achieve them.

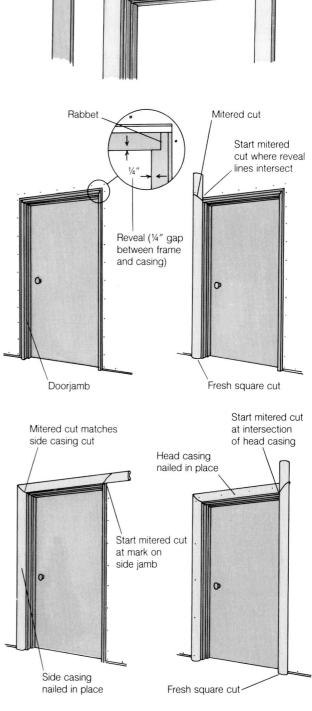

Rabbet

Reveal (¼" gap between frame and casing)

¼"

Doorjamb

Mitered cut

Start mitered cut where reveal lines intersect

Fresh square cut

Mitered cut matches side casing cut

Start mitered cut at mark on side jamb

Side casing nailed in place

Start mitered cut at intersection of head casing

Head casing nailed in place

Fresh square cut

Lock Nailing

When a mitered joint is slightly off, this method can often be used to close the gap. It works because the trim wood is usually flexible. First, squeeze some glue into the crack. Then drive a casing nail through the head casing into the side casing, and another nail from the side casing into the head casing, as shown on page 36. Wipe away any excess glue immediately and sand lightly when dry.

Coping a Mitered Joint

When you work with molded casing, some of which is thick and elaborate, the joints must always be mitered so that the molding will stay in a consistent line. For a tight joint in this case, the back of one mitered piece must be beveled. Turn the casing over and use a coping saw to cut a thin scallop of wood from the back. Coping is necessary on only one side of a mitered joint.

Exterior Trim

Weathering damages out-of-door trim, but there are some things that you can do to protect it. For an informal look (or perhaps to match existing trim), you might use rough-sawn lumber finished with a stain. This is a fairly forgiving, durable finish. For painted trim select your material more carefully. Lumberyards carry the smaller trim sizes in many shapes, and the wood is usually kiln dried. It is very important that whatever material you use be kiln dried. Otherwise you'll get a lot of opening at the joints from shrinkage, and the paint

may fail as the trapped moisture tries to escape. Many painters recommend back priming and painting the trim to increase the durability of the paint job. If you prefer a clear finish, specify trim lumber that has a vertical grain. It is more expensive than flat-grain lumber, but it will hold up better to sunlight and water. Use stainless steel nails to prevent any possible streaking.

Finally, if you are going to paint the trim and the siding, be sure to caulk the joint between them well. If there is caulk under the door trim, and if it is properly flashed, you can caulk the outside joint adequately with a siliconized acrylic.

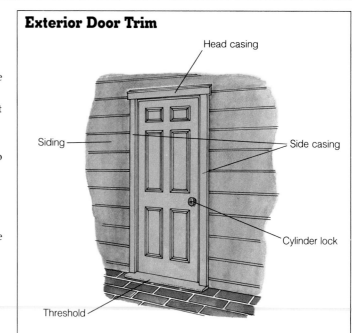

Exterior Door Trim

Head casing

Siding

Side casing

Cylinder lock

Threshold

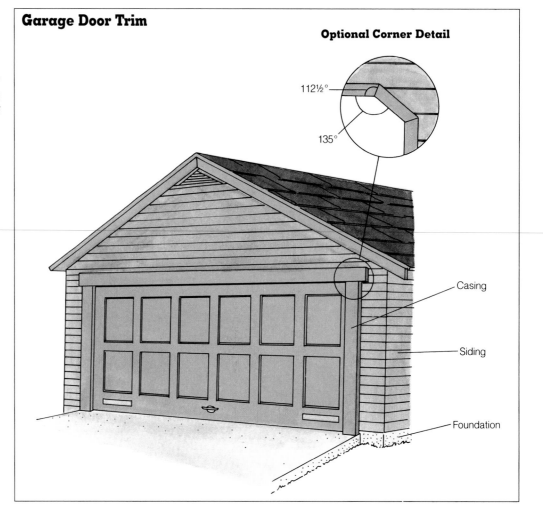

Garage Door Trim

Optional Corner Detail

112½°

135°

Casing

Siding

Foundation

SOME SPECIAL TYPES OF DOORS

Special situations call for special types of doors. Inside the house, bifold, pocket, and bypass doors save space in tight quarters. On the exterior, garage, basement, and pet doors provide needed access. This section discusses the special considerations involved in installing each type of door.

Bifold Doors

In places where a conventional door would just be in the way, a bifold unit comes to the rescue. When open, bifold doors fit neatly against the jambs; when closed, they provide a warm and interesting break in the wall. They are commonly louvered to reduce weight and increase ventilation, but some models have a hollow core. A big advantage of bifold doors is that they are quickly installed in an existing doorframe.

Bifolds come in different widths. A single unit consists of two doors hinged together. For large openings use two units of equal size.

You cannot always find doors to fit your openings exactly. When the doorway is too narrow for the doors, trim them down with a plane or a table saw. When the doorway is too wide, trim it out with stock of a thickness sufficient to make the doors fit.

The hardware for bifold doors consists of an overhead track that contains a top pivot; a bottom pivot; a slide guide; aligners; and an adjusting bolt at the bottom of the door to raise or lower it. If you already have the doors, you can buy just the hardware, or you can buy the doors and the hardware as a kit.

Installing Bifold Doors

Measure the width of the door opening. If necessary, cut the overhead track to fit with a hacksaw. Place the track in the center of the head jamb and mark the center of the pre-drilled screw holes. Take the track down and drill the holes in the head jamb.

Next, insert the rubber bumper on the door-closing side of the track. For a pair of doors that close in the middle, slide the bumper to the center of the track, so that it will cushion the doors when they close. Slip the top pivot bracket on the end of the track. For a pair of doors, slip brackets on both ends. Then screw the track to the head jamb.

Push the top pivot bracket (or brackets) against the door-way, but don't tighten the holding screw yet. Drop a plumb bob from the end of the track and position the bottom pivot bracket directly under the

Installing Bifold Doors

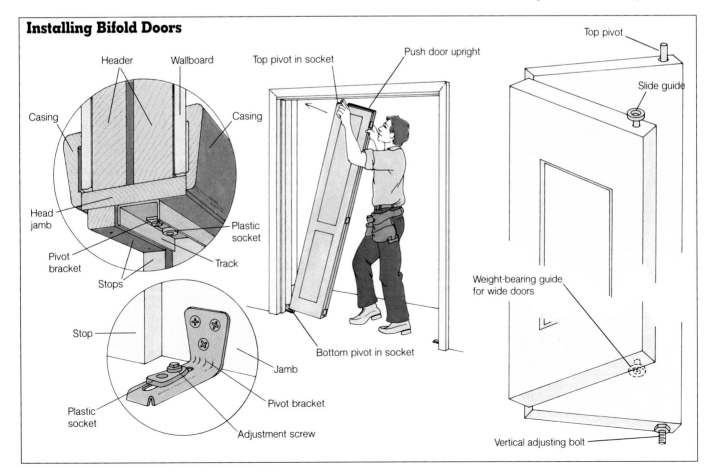

Header · Wallboard · Top pivot in socket · Push door upright · Top pivot
Casing · Casing · Slide guide
Head jamb · Plastic socket
Pivot bracket · Track · Stops
Stop · Jamb · Plastic socket · Pivot bracket · Adjustment screw · Bottom pivot in socket
Weight-bearing guide for wide doors
Vertical adjusting bolt

top one. For a pair of doors, do this at each end. Screw the brackets to the wall and to the floor. If carpeting is to be installed, cut a strip of plywood to fit under each bottom bracket thick enough to raise it slightly above the carpet. Insert the vertical adjusting bolt into the bottom of each door; drill holes if necessary. Drill the top of each door and insert the top pivot and slide guide, as illustrated on page 39.

Top: Bifold doors needn't be plain; this set, with an oak surface, matches the adjacent passage door and gives the look of recessed paneling.
Bottom: A variation of the bifold door, this accordion-fold door allows the pass-through to be opened for convenience, or closed to separate formal from casual rooms.

Attach the doors one at a time as follows. First, set the bottom pivot into the bottom socket. Tilt the door toward the center of the opening and slide its top pivot bracket over to the center of the track. Push the door all the way back to the jamb, check that it is vertical, and tighten the holding screws on the top and bottom brackets. Open the door and raise or lower it as necessary by turning the vertical adjusting bolt. Also do this with the other door, if you are installing a pair.

Now install the trim around the door (see pages 36 and 37).

Close the doors and screw the metal door aligners in place on the back face of each door about 8 inches from the bottom. Place an aligner at one side for a single door or in the middle for a pair of doors.

Sliding Closet Doors

Sliding doors, often referred to as bypass doors, are commonly used on closets because they are inexpensive and easy to install. You can use virtually any type of door, plain or louvered. Some models are mirrored, which can enhance the decor of the bedroom. These heavier doors are installed like sliding glass doors.

The basic hardware for sliding closet doors consists of an overhead track, a pair of wheels that attach to the top of each door, and door guides that are fastened to the floor. Better-quality hardware will include a floor track with rollers built into it that guide the doors smoothly. The floor track is desirable, especially with heavy doors; without it the doors will tend to rattle. You can buy the hardware separately and use inexpensive hollow-core doors, or buy the doors and the hardware in a kit.

The doors should be 1½ inches less in height than the opening. This allows 1¼ inches at the top for the track and ¼ inch of clearance above the floor or carpet. The latter is not a critical measurement, because the doors can be raised or lowered with adjusting screws on the wheel, as illustrated. Each door should be ½ inch wider than half the opening, so that they overlap by 1 inch when closed. If you can't get doors of the proper width, trim the edges with a power saw guided by a fence (a straight board clamped to the door) to narrow them, or add trim to the inside of the doorway to decrease the size of the opening.

Installing the Door

Most overhead tracks are adjustable. Place the track against the head jamb, open it until it touches both side jambs, mark through the predrilled holes, and drill the screw holes. Install the track with the channels that carry the wheels facing into the closet. Mount a pair of wheels on the top edge of each door. Place them about 2 inches in from each end. With the overhead track up and the wheels mounted on the doors, hang the inside door on the inside channel first. Then hang the outside door. Check

Installing Bypass Doors

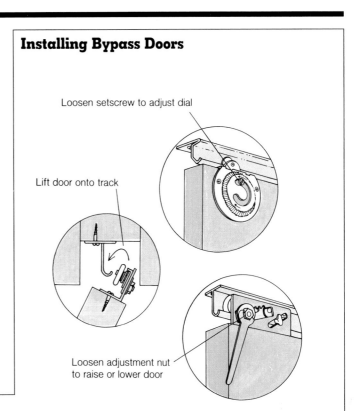

Loosen setscrew to adjust dial

Lift door onto track

Loosen adjustment nut to raise or lower door

Note: Doors will have either an adjustment nut or an adjustment dial

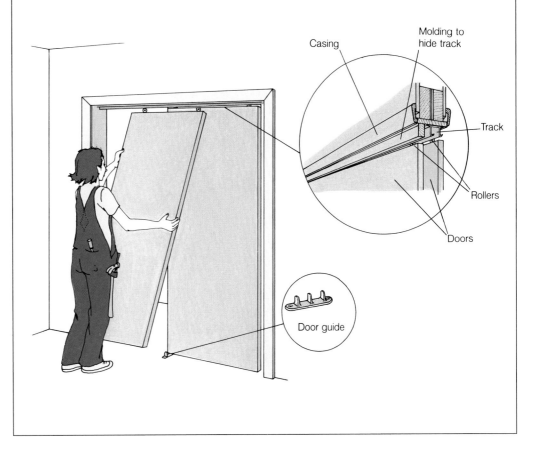

Casing

Molding to hide track

Track

Rollers

Doors

Door guide

how straight the doors hang by pushing them back and comparing them to the jambs, which should be plumb. If a door is hanging crooked, loosen the adjusting screw on the roller from the back (see detail on page 41) and raise or lower the door until it rides on the rollers. If you are installing a floor track, remove the doors, screw the track to the floor, and replace the doors.

If the hardware does not include a floor track, you can help to keep the doors from swinging and banging into each other by installing a metal or plastic floor guide. Screw the guide to the floor between the doors in the center of the opening where they meet. If the guide is adjustable, as they usually are, move the side pieces until it clears the doors by ⅛ inch.

Finally, install the trim around the doors (see pages 36 and 37).

Pocket Doors

There are two ways to buy a pocket door. You can purchase a complete, ready-made unit, or you can buy just the hardware and add the door of your choice.

The ready-made units are sold in a variety of standard widths; they are all 80 inches high. Kits that supply just the hardware include an adjustable overhead track, wheels that attach to the top of the door and fit in the track, a split jamb, and a split stud.

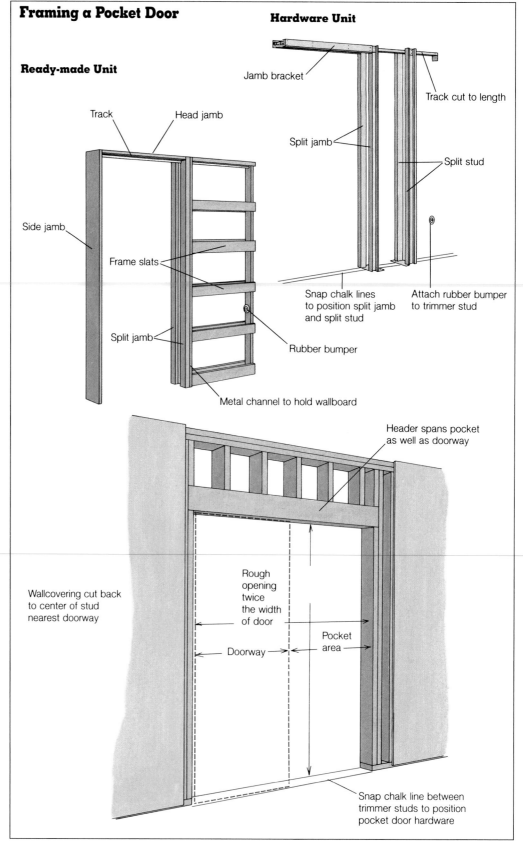

Framing a Pocket Door

Ready-made Unit

Track
Head jamb
Side jamb
Frame slats
Split jamb
Metal channel to hold wallboard
Rubber bumper

Hardware Unit

Jamb bracket
Track cut to length
Split jamb
Split stud
Snap chalk lines to position split jamb and split stud
Attach rubber bumper to trimmer stud

Header spans pocket as well as doorway
Wallcovering cut back to center of stud nearest doorway
Rough opening twice the width of door
Pocket area
Doorway
Snap chalk line between trimmer studs to position pocket door hardware

Installing Pocket Doors

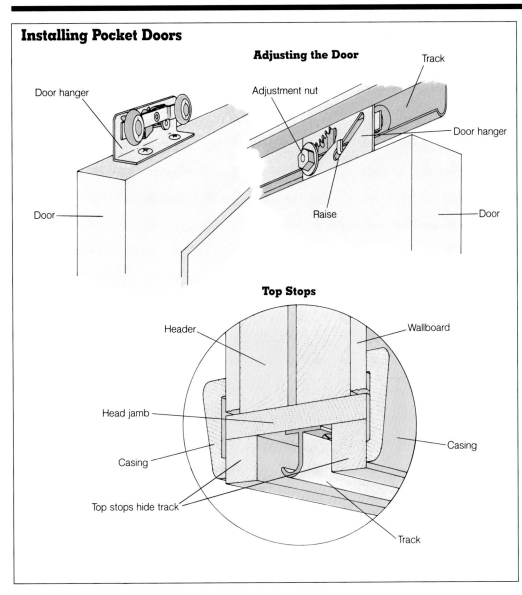

Adjusting the Door

Door hanger

Track

Adjustment nut

Door hanger

Door

Raise

Door

Top Stops

Header

Wallboard

Head jamb

Casing

Casing

Top stops hide track

Track

Preparing the Opening

The first step in installing a pocket door in an existing wall is to remove the paneling or wallboard. Determine where you want the opening to be. Position the latch side of the door against an existing stud, if possible. From there measure across the wall twice the width of the opening. Find the nearest stud beyond that point,

snap a chalk line down the center, and cut the wallboard along that line. Snap another chalk line over the center of the stud at the latch side of the door and repeat the process. Take down the wallboard and remove the intervening studs by sawing them and pulling them out. Cut near the top and bottom so that you can reuse them in framing the door. If any nails remain, cut them flush to the plate using nippers

or a hacksaw. If you are turning an existing doorway into a pocket door, remove the door framing material, including the header.

Using the methods described on pages 19 and 23, install new trimmer studs and a new header. The bottom of the header should be about 1½ inches above the door, to leave room for the track. Plumb and square the opening.

Installing Ready-made Units

The ready-made unit is the easiest type of pocket door to install. It comes with a hollow-core door inside the frame slats, to which the head jamb, side jamb, and overhead track are taped. The illustration shows how it looks when the pieces are assembled.

When the opening is ready, remove the door, jambs, and track and put the frame in the pocket. Check that it is plumb and level. Then nail it to the trimmer stud.

Now mount the wheels on the top of the door about 1 inch from each end.

Nail the side jamb to the trimmer stud on the latch side of the opening. Then install the head jamb at the top. Level and stiffen the head jamb by placing shims between it and the header. Nail it to the header through the shims.

Screw the overhead track to the head jamb, being careful to keep it centered. Lift the door and hook the wheels onto the track. Adjust the wheels until the door just clears the floor or carpet and hangs straight when closed.

Re-cover the studs with wallboard or paneling. Then trim out the doorway.

Installing Adjustable Units

First, place the overhead track in the opening and extend it until both ends butt against the trimmer studs. Check to make sure that it is centered and level. Then nail it at each end to the trimmer studs.

Snap chalk lines on the floor between the outer edges of the trimmer studs. Place one chalk line on each side of the opening. These are guides for positioning the split jamb and the split stud in the pocket.

Place the split jamb at the edge of the opening. Screw the top to the overhead track. Check the split jamb for plumb with a level. Then screw the bottom to the floor (the screws go through the tab at the bottom of the split jamb). If everything is positioned correctly, the split jamb should be centered between the chalk lines while it is plumb.

Install the split stud in the same manner as the split jamb.

Gliding Mechanism

The door is hung as follows. First, mount the wheels to the door and hang it on the track, adjusting the wheel mechanisms to make the door the proper height.

Install door guides at the base of the split jamb, adjusting them to allow ⅛ inch of clearance from the door.

Install the bumper where the midpoint of the door will hit it. Adjust the bumper with shims or washers so that the door will extend ⅜ inch beyond the split jamb when it is recessed.

Cover the exposed trimmer stud with jamb stock and the framing with wallboard.

Use 1⅛-inch doorstop material to conceal the track and the split jambs. Leave ⅛ inch of clearance on both sides.

Finally, trim the opening with casing material (see pages 36 and 37).

Installing Garage Doors

If you want to bring home the correct garage door, make sure you've measured the opening properly. In addition to the opening, measure the distances from the opening to the interior sidewalls and the ceiling. You will need all of these measurements in order to make sure that there is enough room for the tracks and the opener equipment.

Garage door openings are usually standard in size. However, you may need to alter yours to make it fit the door you want. If you are widening the opening, it is crucial to have a big enough header. Consult a professional to determine what size header you need and refer back to the section on structural preparations and shoring (pages 18 to 25).

Be very careful when you remove the old door. The springs can be under great tension, and they could fly off and injure you. If you cannot tell whether the springs are under tension, ask a professional to look at them.

Garage doors are usually very easy to install. Manufacturers compete for your business by taking great pains to provide foolproof instructions. Just follow normal safety precautions, and if you do have a question, use the manufacturer's toll-free number to get a quick answer.

When you have installed the door, be sure to grease the tracks for smooth operation. You'll also want to clean the tracks and rollers periodically. Finally, if you have added an opener to an existing door, be sure to jam the existing door locks in the *open* position or else remove them. The motor of the opener will be seriously damaged if it strains to open a door that has been accidentally locked.

Installing Pet Doors

Pet doors come with complete installation instructions. Usually the pet door itself can be used as a template to mark the house door for cutting. Drill a hole at each corner of the cutout and then remove the rest of the material using a jigsaw or a saber saw. You may want to cover the base of the saw with masking tape to avoid marring the surface of the house door. It's not a bad idea to put some caulk under the top and side edges of the outside face of the pet door when you install it.

If you are installing the pet door in a wall, first be sure that there are no wires or pipes where you intend to put it. If you can't tell, make a small hole and enlarge it gingerly until you are sure that the area is clear. See the section on creating new door openings (page 22). You can build a small rectangular liner for the space between the outside and the inside wall out of ¼-inch plywood. It will be held in place by the flanges on the inner and outer sections of the pet door.

When installing the kind of pet door that fits into a sliding glass door, be sure to caulk the unit as instructed. These units usually come with a new locking mechanism to replace the one that gets covered up by the pet door panel. Be sure that it is of good quality. If it isn't, replace it with one that is.

Installing Basement Doors

Installation is simple. Just screw the frame down to the concrete curb, using lead anchors to hold the screws in their holes. Make sure that you have caulked under the bottom of the door unit and also that some provision has been made to keep water from running down the face of the wall above the door and getting behind the top of the door frame where it touches the building. A Z flashing that extends under the siding and over the top of the unit may be the answer.

Creating an Outside Entrance

An outside entrance enhances any basement and is well worth the effort to build it. The most difficult step is breaching the basement wall, especially if it is reinforced concrete. In that case it is better to have the wall cut by a professional concrete sawing contractor. You can rent a jackhammer to help you break through other types of walls.

Building the Areaway

Although you only need enough space for a set of stairs, build as large an outside areaway as you can. It will make an extra window possible and create a more pleasant entry. A large, terraced opening creates a feeling of luxury and is not as difficult to build as an areaway with retaining walls, but if you do not have the space you can follow this procedure for a steep-walled entry.

Excavate a hole large enough for the areaway plus retaining walls, to a depth 4 inches below the foundation floor. If you plan concrete steps, leave a ramp along one edge of the hole on which to pour the steps.

Dig footing trenches for the retaining walls 16 inches wide to a depth that matches the foundation footings.

Set two horizontal rebars in the trench, at least 3 inches from the soil. Tie vertical rebars to the horizontal bars at appropriate intervals so they will line up inside concrete block cavities. Then pour a concrete footing 8 inches deep in the trench.

Install a drainage line around the exterior of the footing and tie it into the main foundation drain.

Build a concrete block wall to grade level or slightly higher. Start at the corners and fill in between.

Apply waterproofing to the outside surface of the block wall. Use asphalt emulsion,

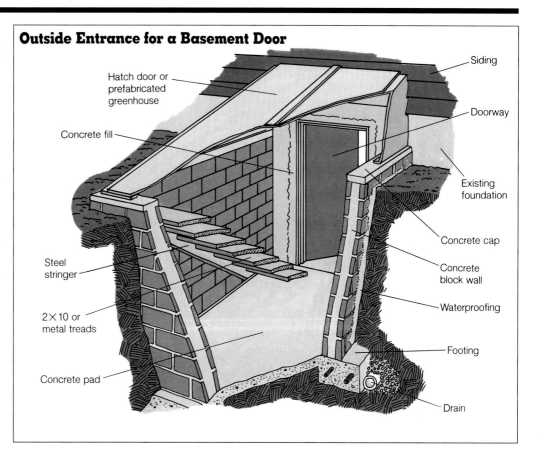

Outside Entrance for a Basement Door

- Hatch door or prefabricated greenhouse
- Concrete fill
- Steel stringer
- 2 × 10 or metal treads
- Concrete pad
- Siding
- Doorway
- Existing foundation
- Concrete cap
- Concrete block wall
- Waterproofing
- Footing
- Drain

bentonite, a rigid membrane, or another method recommended for local conditions.

Breaching the Foundation Wall

Mark cutting lines on the inside of the basement wall for a hole large enough for the doorway and frame. Starting from the inside should reduce rubble in the basement.

Shore up floor joists for any opening wider than 3 feet, or as necessary. Break through the wall with power tools, hammer and chisel, or sledgehammer. Make the edges as clean and smooth as possible.

Installing the Door

Position an exterior doorframe into the opening. Temporarily brace it after making sure it is plumb and level.

Fill the area between the frame and the wall with cement mortar or concrete topping before installing the door in the frame.

Building the Stairs

Because of possible weather exposure and the need for a fire escape, the stairway should be concrete, masonry, or steel prefabricated for exterior use.

Concrete and masonry stairs can be incorporated into the retaining walls. Leave a wide

ramp along one wall as you excavate and build the stairs on top of it, using standard forming techniques for concrete stairs. Prefabricated steel stringers are available for basement entrances; installation instructions are included.

Covering the Areaway

For an all-weather entrance, cover the stairway with a hatch door or shelter. A prefabricated greenhouse makes an attractive entry and provides extra light to the basement.

For either type of enclosure, form and pour a concrete cap on top of the block retaining walls. The final height depends on the height needed for the stairs and the type of enclosure.

STORM AND SCREEN DOORS

Storm doors create a dead-air space that inhibits the flow of cold air and the loss of heat. Screen doors, which provide warm-weather protection against insects, are structurally similar to storm doors and are installed in the same manner.

Choosing Storm and Screen Doors

Storm doors may be made of wood, in which case they are installed like a prehung door (see pages 26 and 27). The instructions that follow are for the more common aluminum-frame door. These instructions also apply to combination storm-and-screen doors, in which the upper glass panel can be replaced with a screen during warm weather.

Before you purchase a storm door, measure the width of the door opening. A snug fit is necessary if the storm door is to be effective. When shopping compare the price of a purchased storm door with the cost of having one custom-made. The difference may not be that great, and a custom-made door will give you a tighter fit.

Screen doors are available in a large number of styles to complement almost any type of architecture. The simple aluminum door is still commonly available; more recently, manufacturers have added ornate wooden screen doors to their lines. Be sure to inspect the workmanship of a wooden screen door before you buy it. Also, make sure the hinge design will work with your existing doorjamb.

Security screen doors are also available. These usually have metal screening with a metal reinforcing grille. The grilles on some security models are decorative, so the doors offer resistance against break-ins without giving the house a fortress-like appearance.

A self-closing mechanism is a convenient feature. A cylinder mounted at the top of the door pulls it slowly shut. The mechanism includes a latching device that allows the screen door to be propped open. A self-closing mechanism may be included with a particular screen door, or you may have to buy it separately.

Screen Door Styles

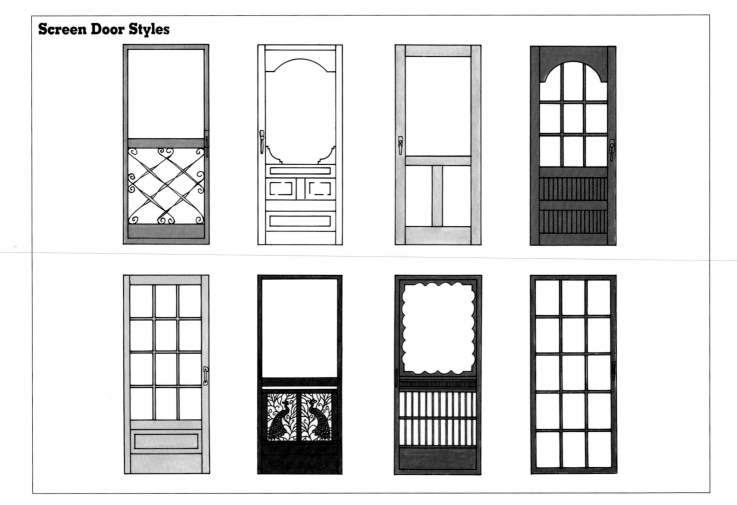

Installing Storm and Screen Doors

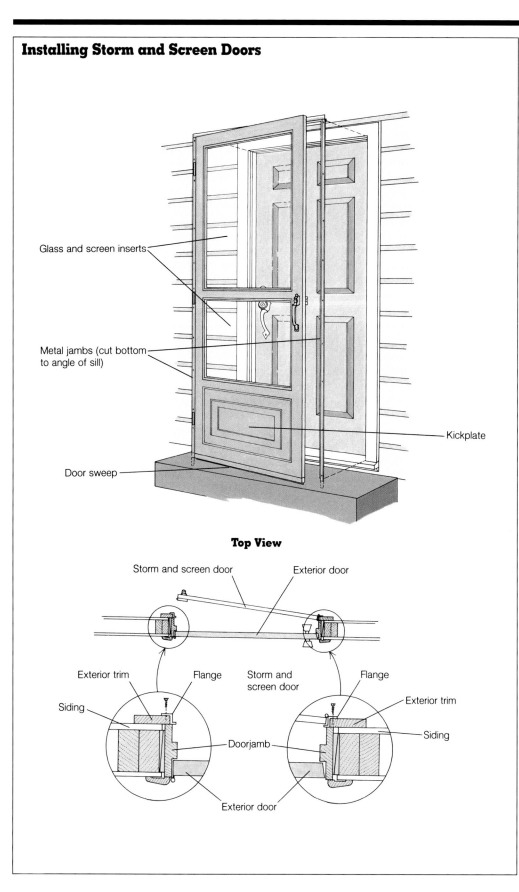

Glass and screen inserts

Metal jambs (cut bottom to angle of sill)

Door sweep

Kickplate

Top View

Storm and screen door

Exterior door

Exterior trim

Flange

Siding

Storm and screen door

Flange

Exterior trim

Siding

Doorjamb

Exterior door

Installing Storm and Screen Doors

These doors are fairly simple to install, but some cutting may be required. The door is shipped fully assembled, with hinges in place. However, the metal jambs are often left several inches longer than the door, so that you can cut them to fit the opening. Do this with a hacksaw, cutting at an angle to match the slope of the door-sill. To make the cuts, you may have to remove the adjustable sweep at the bottom of the storm door.

Place the door in the opening and shim at each bottom corner until it is centered and square. Note how the Z-shaped flanges on the jambs fit over the exterior trim. When the door is centered and square, drill pilot holes in the trim through the flange holes and screw the flange to the trim.

If the door is equipped with a door sweep, open the door and lower the sweep until it makes contact with the sill. Tighten the screws to hold it in place.

Following the manufacturer's instructions, install the latch and the self-closing mechanism.

WINDOWS

Windows provide the opportunity to transform a house. With good planning, moderate effort, and the techniques described in this chapter, do-it-yourselfers can bring about a vast improvement in the appearance and energy efficiency of a home. The chapter discusses the traditional functions of windows—that is, admitting light, air, and the view. It will help you to plan the integration of windows into a house. It describes the many new features you will find in today's windows, and it tells where to shop for them, how to purchase them, and how to install them.

Different window shapes can be combined to fit almost any room. Here, the semicircular upper window complements the peak of the ceiling, and the rectangular windows provide an open feeling.

DESIGN AND PLANNING

New windows can improve the appearance, energy efficiency, and security of the home. Careful thought before you buy will ensure that you get the most from these benefits.

Selecting the Style

New windows should maintain or improve the overall aesthetics of your home. Pick a style that harmonizes with the existing windows. For instance, it's usually best to avoid using wood and metal windows in the same house. If you are replacing all of the windows in the house, you'll have more latitude, but your choice should still harmonize with the style of the exterior. Metal casement windows might be most appropriate on a contemporary house; a colonial-style home might look best with wood double-hung windows. Spend some time sketching and visualizing before you choose.

Windows are available in a large variety of configurations. One of the best-known traditional designs is the double-hung window. It has two sashes, which move past each other vertically. Older units also have sash weights and cords to keep the sash stationary when it is opened. These windows are attractive, but they do require a lot of maintenance to prevent them from sticking. They also tend to leak air.

Many improvements have been incorporated into modern double-hung windows. The cords and sash weights have been replaced by the spring lift and the spring balance;

weather stripping is up-to-date and effective; and there are models with sashes that tilt into the room, making cleaning much easier. Double-hung

windows are available in metal, wood, and vinyl. There are also single-hung versions, usually with a fixed top sash.

Sliding windows are popular, particularly in newer buildings. Some of the less costly models are of low quality, but sliding windows of very good quality are available. Tracks and hardware operate smoothly, and these units

come with most of the other features that you would expect to find in a modern window.

Casement windows are hinged on the left or right side. They are operated either by releasing a lever and pushing the sash outward or by turning a crank. Most modern casements use a crank. Hopper and awning styles have similar mechanisms, but hoppers open

With eye-catching shapes above and awning windows for ventilation below, this window wall combines beauty and practicality. Framing the openings for unique installations such as this requires the help of a qualified professional.

Window Types and Shapes

Fixed-Pane

Casement

Double-Hung

Sliding

Awning/Hopper

Combining Window Shapes

at the top, and awning windows open at the bottom. Hoppers and awnings encourage good ventilation throughout the house.

Jalousie windows, with their many small panes of glass, also provide good ventilation, but they are difficult to clean and are tremendously drafty. They can be used in a warm climate, but for the most part they are out of style today.

Less common designs include the rotating window, which pivots on a central axis. It is easy to clean, since it can be turned 360 degrees. Many manufacturers will also combine different styles of windows to create large custom units. For instance, you might get a large fixed window with two narrow hoppers or awnings below, or a row of alternating fixed and casement windows.

Double-hung windows generally don't mix well with other styles. This tends to be true of sliding windows, too, although sliders can be combined with large fixed windows. Casements, awnings, and hoppers usually have the same sash cross section. They can be combined with one another and with fixed units. However, this is just a general guide. Don't be afraid to experiment a bit. Sometimes a different style thrown in as an accent can work very well.

Light and Ventilation

In choosing windows think about climate and exposure. One nice feature of awning windows, for example, is that they will shed water if you open them in rainy weather. This may be useful if you live in a warm, humid climate. On the other hand, if you like the look of low hoppers around the room, they will work well—provided you live in the dry Southwest. Similarly, casements can be oriented so that when they are open they either scoop air into the room or protect the opening from a prevailing breeze.

Each style of window is screened a bit differently too. Double-hung units are screened on the outside, so the screen does not affect the operation of the window. Sliding windows can also be screened on the outside. Casements, hoppers, and awnings all open to the outside, however, so the screen must be placed inside

---

Considering the Sun in Placing Windows

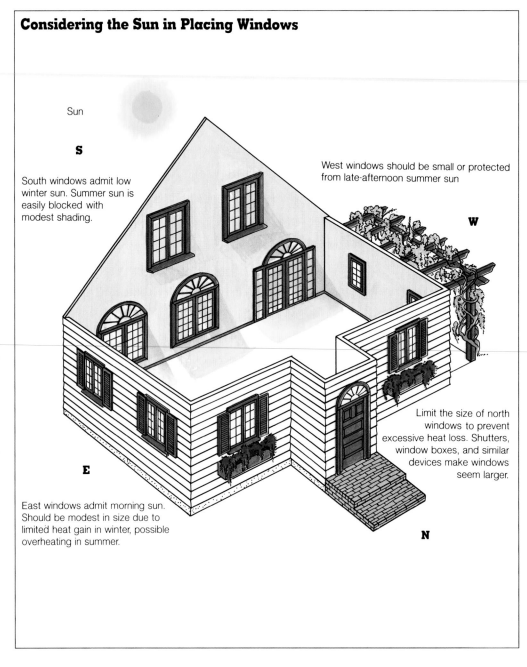

Sun

S

South windows admit low winter sun. Summer sun is easily blocked with modest shading.

West windows should be small or protected from late-afternoon summer sun

W

E

East windows admit morning sun. Should be modest in size due to limited heat gain in winter, possible overheating in summer.

Limit the size of north windows to prevent excessive heat loss. Shutters, window boxes, and similar devices make windows seem larger.

N

the room. This introduces the problem of how to open and shut the window. To work well with screens, these windows should be crank-operated. Manufacturers sometimes place a little door in the screen to allow you to get at the latch mechanism, if there is one.

Windows admit sunlight as well as air. Some modern designs control the amount and kind of light they admit. Coatings for glass can keep out damaging UV radiation and help to stop heat loss through the windows. These coatings are discussed in detail on page 54.

Consider solar gain when you plan new windows. In most climates new glass should be located on the south side of the building whenever possible. Modern units keep heat in; you may be surprised at how warm your house can be with thoughtfully placed, energy-efficient windows. This effect can be increased by positioning the windows so that the sun strikes some material that can absorb heat, which is then radiated back into the house at night. One way to do this is to have a tile floor near the windows, best of all with a few inches of concrete under it. Another way is to have heavier walls in that part of the house, finished either with a double layer of wallboard, or better yet, with plaster.

You should also consider the placement of the windows with respect to their compass orientation and to the overhang of the eaves. Eaves can work to your advantage if you place the windows so that the overhang blocks the high, hot summer sun but allows the low winter sun to strike the windows and warm the interior of the house.

Finally, check the local building code to see whether it limits the amount of window area you can add to your home. To encourage energy conservation, some localities have such regulations. The allowable square footage of glazing is usually expressed as a percentage of the floor area of the house.

Security

Most of today's windows resist break-ins much better than their predecessors did. The popular aluminum slider sometimes had flimsy locks; its particular weak point was that the sash could easily be removed. If you are buying sliding wood or metal windows, check to see that the locking hardware is sturdy, and that some provision has been made to prevent the sash from being lifted out of the track.

Casements, awnings, and hoppers usually have very strong latching devices. They are not easy to pry open without actually breaking the sash or the glass. The individual panes of jalousie windows can sometimes be easily slid out of their frames.

Avoid putting small panes of glass in locations where a person could reach through them and open a door or window. In the case of an exterior door, do not deal with this problem by using a double-cylinder dead bolt (one that is keyed from the inside). Although this was common practice in the past, doors that require a key to operate from the inside pose a very serious hazard in case of fire and violate many safety codes.

A better solution to this problem is to use plastic glazing. Plexiglas and Lexan are two popular choices. These are not completely foolproof, though; a savvy burglar may use a torch to melt the plastic.

If your situation calls for it, you may have to resort to a security grille. Screens are available that have fine electrical wires woven into the mesh and an electrical switch on one edge. They can be connected into an alarm system, so the alarm will go off if the screen is cut or removed. Another option in some locations is to use glass block. This can usually be done in an attractive way. Tempered glass provides a modicum of security in that it makes a tremendous noise when it is broken.

Privacy

It is possible to add light or ventilation while maintaining privacy. Frosted or heavily tinted glazing is available, as is reflective glass, although the latter is not much seen in residential use.

Windows placed high in the room may also provide the desired light or ventilation and maintain privacy. Awnings and hoppers work well in high locations. Some models can be operated with a pole or driven by a motor.

Many window manufacturers have designed shading and blind systems specifically for their products. These can be ordered together with the window or added later.

Safety

Building codes require tempered or safety laminated glass for certain installations—usually for windows less than 18 inches from the floor or within 12 inches of a door. Also, it must be used in doors, including storm doors. Tempered glass breaks into tiny, relatively harmless bits. Safety laminate has a sheet of sticky plastic sandwiched between two sheets of glass; if the window breaks, the glass shards stick to the plastic. It may also be a good idea to use tempered glass in areas where it isn't required, but where someone might trip and fall against the window—for example, in bathrooms or around stairs.

Building codes specify minimum window sizes in rooms used for sleeping. A typical requirement is that each bedroom have at least one window with a minimum clear openable height of 24 inches and a minimum clear openable width of 20 inches. The sill must not be more than 44 inches above the floor. The use of security grilles is also restricted. See the local building code for the most up-to-date information on these requirements.

The building code may also forbid you to cut new windows into a wall facing a property line, unless it is a certain distance from that line. This is a fire safety regulation. Sometimes it can be circumvented by using special fire-rated window assemblies, which are generally made of steel and wire glass. This is a complex issue that varies widely from place to place. Again, refer to the local building code.

SELECTION AND PURCHASE

Shopping for windows can be just as interesting as shopping for doors. Most, but not all, window manufacturers make both, since there is an overlap in the technology involved. Windows are sold at the same places as doors, as well as at specialty stores, and they come in a wide variety of styles and materials.

Where to Shop for Windows

In addition to lumberyards, home-improvement centers, and specialty stores, shop for windows in salvage yards. These are your best bet if you are looking for an accent window—a stained-glass one, for instance—or perhaps one with a bow top. It's tougher than most people realize to recycle old windows for use in a modern home. They may leak unless they are completely reputtied, and you won't find any double glazing in these old beauties. However, that special window may be worth it.

Strategies for purchasing windows are the same as those for buying doors, so reread pages 10 and 11 carefully. Windows are also handled like doors during delivery and on-site. They are a little less prone to warping, but on the other hand, there is a lot of glass you'll need to be careful of.

Materials and Construction

Wood was the first material used for frames in window construction, and it is still one of the most popular. Wood has some great natural advantages, such as its insulating qualities and its inherent beauty. One

of its main disadvantages has been the need for maintenance. This has largely been done away with in modern wood windows. The broken cords and sticky sashes have been replaced by smoothly operating and tightly sealing sliding mechanisms. The old chipped or peeling paint has given way to new coatings, such as polyurea finishes.

A good point to note if you are interested in wood windows: The wood is usually treated with fungicides or preservatives to make it more durable. If anyone in your family is allergic to these products, you can special-order untreated windows from most manufacturers.

Another approach to improving the durability of wood windows is aluminum or vinyl cladding. Aluminum tends to look a bit crisper, but vinyl is superior in areas exposed to salt water or salt air. Cladding is very durable and comes in several colors. If you feel that a clad sash makes the window look too bulky, some manufacturers offer windows with clad jambs and a polyurea finish on the sash.

Modern aluminum windows come in a wide range of styles and quality grades. Features to consider include frames with thermal breaks

(usually plastic inserts) to keep the frame from conducting heat out and cold in, and a wide range of colors to choose from. Look especially at the quality of the rollers on a sliding sash and at the functioning of the locks.

Steel windows are not much used today. Steel is more costly to fabricate than aluminum. However, it does see some use in windows that are designed to provide fire resistance.

Fiberglass and polyvinyl chloride (PVC) are two very interesting new materials for windows. PVC seems to be the more popular. In fact, these windows are generally made of chlorinated polyvinyl chloride (CPVC) and are usually referred to as vinyl windows. They are remarkably durable, and water cannot damage them. They also look attractive. They don't accept paint well, however, so you'll need to stick with the original colors.

Much of modern window technology has centered around the glass itself. One common term is *low-E*, meaning "low emissivity." The low-E characteristic is provided by a microscopically thin layer of metal oxides. This can be coated onto the glass or suspended in the space between the panes of a double-pane window. The coating allows most visible light to pass through, while heat is reflected back into the house.

Short-wavelength rays from the sun, which provide visible light, pass through the low-E coating. When these waves strike the floor, furniture, or other objects, they break into longer waves, which provide heat. The long waves are reflected back into the room by

the low-E coating. This works conversely in the summer. The long-wave heat radiating up from walks and driveways is reflected back off the windows instead of passing through them into the house.

Low-E glass, when used in a double-pane insulated unit, is a formidable saver of energy. Manufacturers also claim that low-E glass stops a certain amount of ultraviolet (UV) radiation (which causes fading). However, there are other coatings that are designed especially to cut down on UV, and also to cut back on visible light. You may have seen bronze-coated windows; today gray-tinted windows are also very popular. They still cut back on light, but they don't look as dark or affect the quality of the light passing through them as much as the bronze ones.

Manufacturers have found that they can increase insulating quality, or R-value, by removing the air from between the panes of an insulated unit. Argon, a dense, inert gas, is usually injected into the space. Some manufacturers use insulating gels; others use a soft coating on a thin polyester film suspended between the two panes.

Each manufacturer uses slightly different combinations of these various processes and features. Comparing them will take time and patience. Be sure to compare figures for R-value. Look for coatings designed to block UV and check test results for the windows. Ask what kinds of tints are available. It's important to see a window that has exactly the combination of features you are considering, to make sure that the quality of light that comes through is just what you expected.

Window Construction and Materials

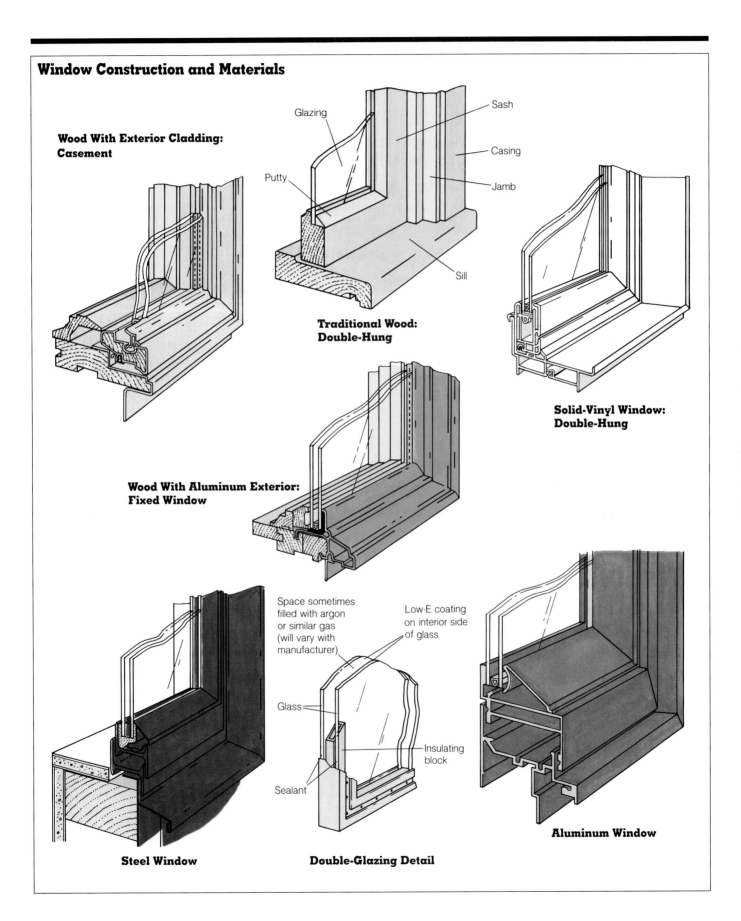

Wood With Exterior Cladding: Casement

Glazing

Putty

Sash

Casing

Jamb

Sill

Traditional Wood: Double-Hung

Solid-Vinyl Window: Double-Hung

Wood With Aluminum Exterior: Fixed Window

Space sometimes filled with argon or similar gas (will vary with manufacturer)

Low-E coating on interior side of glass

Glass

Insulating block

Sealant

Steel Window

Double-Glazing Detail

Aluminum Window

STRUCTURAL PREPARATIONS

The framing alterations necessary for installing windows are similar to those for doors. This section discusses the differences between framing a window opening and framing a door opening. Before you start to work, read the sections on framing (pages 18 to 25) and door installation (pages 26 and 27).

Making the Opening

In some ways a window opening can be simpler to deal with than a door opening. You don't have to deal with a threshold, for example. Nor is it likely that you will have to move wiring, since house wiring is usually run below the level of the windowsills.

The additional framing is not complicated. First, frame the opening as if it were a door. Be sure to leave the bottom plate intact if you are working on an old wall.

Install a rough sill and support it with cripple studs. Toenail the cripple studs at the bottom and facenail one cripple stud against the trimmer on each side. Then cut and install the sill. It is good practice to double the sill on wide openings in order to stiffen the window. The double sill also provides backing for nailing on certain kinds of window trim. In some parts of the country, it is standard practice always to use a double sill. Check the local building code.

Lining Up the Trim

If you are installing windows and doors at the same time, consider how the door and window trim will line up horizontally, both inside and outside the house. A continuous line across the tops of the doors and windows can be difficult to achieve, especially if they come from different manufacturers, or if you are trying to match existing windows and doors. This is because the cross sections of door and window head jambs are not consistent from one manufacturer to the next. Therefore, if you align the upper edges of the head trim, the lower edges may not line up. The only way to deal with this is on a case-by-case basis. Measure the trim pieces, see whether they line up, and adjust accordingly.

Altering an Existing Opening

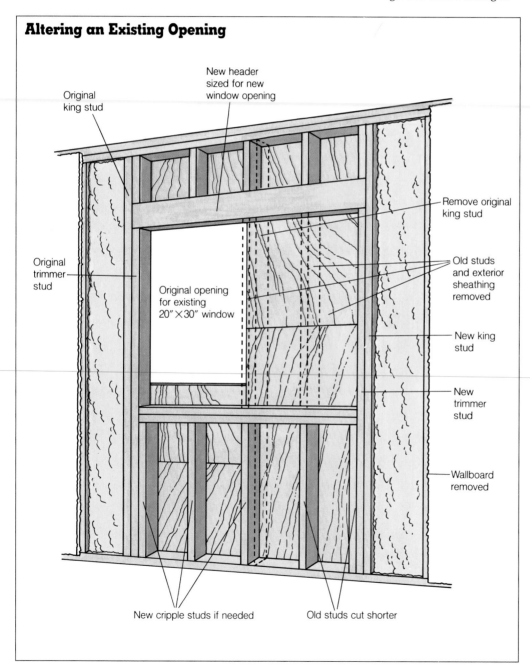

New header sized for new window opening

Original king stud

Original trimmer stud

Original opening for existing 20" × 30" window

Remove original king stud

Old studs and exterior sheathing removed

New king stud

New trimmer stud

Wallboard removed

New cripple studs if needed

Old studs cut shorter

Window Opening in Platform-Style House

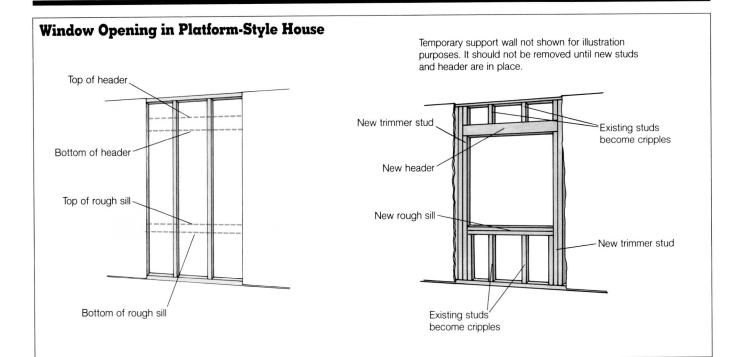

Top of header

Bottom of header

Top of rough sill

Bottom of rough sill

Temporary support wall not shown for illustration purposes. It should not be removed until new studs and header are in place.

New trimmer stud

New header

New rough sill

Existing studs become cripples

New trimmer stud

Existing studs become cripples

A greenhouse room lets you add a great deal of glass with relatively little structural preparation.

Removing a Double-Hung Window

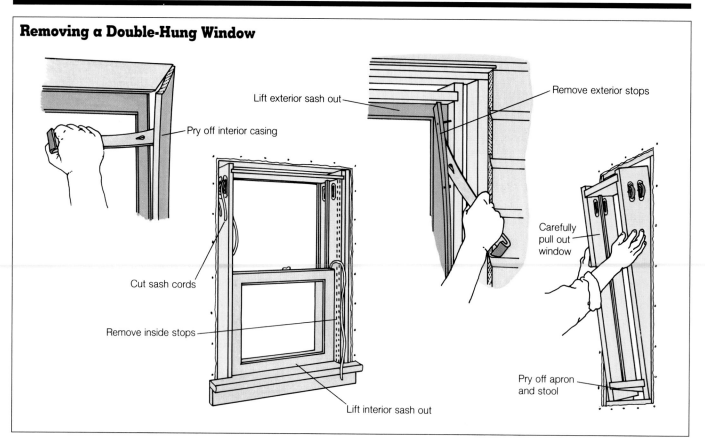

Pry off interior casing

Lift exterior sash out

Remove exterior stops

Cut sash cords

Carefully pull out window

Remove inside stops

Lift interior sash out

Pry off apron and stool

Extending the kitchen counter into a bay window adds useful space with little change to the structure of the house.

Removing an Existing Window

It's best to have the new window on hand before you remove the old one. However, to order the new window, you will need the exact measurements of the rough opening. Start by taking off the inside casing. With the rough opening revealed, measure the width (the distance between the inner edges of the trimmer studs) and the height (the distance between the rough sill and the bottom of the header). Since the opening may not be square, take several measurements.

The new window must fit within the narrowest dimensions. Obtain the new window before you finish removing the old one.

Removing a Wood-Framed Window

The following instructions, which apply specifically to removing a double-hung window, are generally applicable to any wood-framed unit. Work carefully to protect the wood, particularly any trim that you intend to reuse.

A double-hung window can be removed from inside or outside the house, whichever is more convenient. Start by removing the interior window trim. Carefully tap a broad chisel under one edge and gently pry it out. Don't pry it all the way out at first; work your way slowly upward, prying a little at a time, to avoid breaking the trim. If any nails are pulled through the trim and left in the studs, remove them with a claw hammer.

Push both windows down. If the windows are hung by cords, cut them. If there is a spring-loaded balance, twist the metal top to loosen it. Then use the chisel to pry off the interior stops and lift the interior sash out of the frame.

Working from inside, or from outside if convenient, pry off the exterior trim. Again, work carefully if the trim is to be reused. Then remove the exterior stops. On spring-loaded sash balances, twist the metal top, pull it off, and remove the spring. Take out the exterior sash.

Pry off the apron and the stool. Pry off the jambs, if possible. It is sometimes easier to use a nail set to drive the nails through the jambs and sill and then to lift out the window frame as a unit.

Removing a Nailing-Fin Window

Almost all windows held in a metal frame, including fixed, casement, awning, jalousie, and rotating types, have nailing fins. These surround the exterior part of the frame. The frame is placed in the rough opening and the fins are nailed to the trimmer studs, rough sill, and header. Siding covers the fins. Trim covers the gap between the siding and the window.

To remove nailing-fin windows, first pry off all the exterior trim. Work carefully so that it can be reused. The nailing fin is usually 1½ inches wide, so measure out 1¾ inches from the window frame all around and mark the outline on the siding.

Set the blade on a circular saw to ⅛ inch deeper than the thickness of the siding. Use a carbide-tipped blade, since you may hit some nails. Cut along the lines; remove and save the pieces of siding. Carefully pry the nails from the fins and lift out the window.

Removing a Metal-Framed Window

Pry off trim

Mark at top edge of top trim

Cut ⅛" deeper than thickness of siding

Mark and cut 1¾" from window frame

Pull out all nails

Carefully lift window out

INSTALLING THE WINDOW

Old-fashioned wood windows were tedious to install. It took a lot of shimming and trimming to get that perfect fit. Today's windows make the job considerably faster and easier. They are installed in much the same way as doors.

Installing Regular Windows

Like doors, windows are generally installed by nailing either right through the trim or through nailing fins. Before you start, check again to make sure that the opening is square. Refer to the discussion of flashing and papering an opening on pages 34 and 35.

The illustration shows a section cut through the top jamb of a window. Note the metal Z flashing. It tucks up under the building or flashing paper, then out over the top of the wood trim, then slightly down over the front face of the trim. No caulk is needed to waterproof this system. Z flashing like this is also used to waterproof horizontal joints in plywood siding or places where horizontal members, such as deck ledgers, are nailed to the side of a building. Because there is no standard thickness for exterior window trim, the Z flashing over the top of a window is usually custom-made at a sheet-metal shop, typically in 10-foot lengths, out of galvanized material. The important point is that water must be kept out of the head jamb by overlapping the various materials properly.

You'll need helpers to get the windows into their openings. Warn them not to scratch the glass or the frames with their tool belts. If a window is awkwardly heavy or large, you can usually remove operable sash fairly easily. Be very careful with windows that are high up. It may be wise to build or rent a scaffold to stand on for the installation. Don't overestimate what you can do from a ladder. If you know that you are going to be dealing with a high installation, see whether you can get windows that have folding nailing fins. These fins lie flat against the unit, so that you can bring it to the opening from inside, place it on the rough sill, slide it out just a bit, and snap the fins into their *open* position. You can then work from inside, and safely from outside on a ladder.

Once you have the unit placed in the rough opening, slide it to either side as necessary to center it. Tack one of the upper corners in place, but do not drive the nails all the way in. Next, level the sill. Check the manufacturer's instructions to see whether shimming is recommended at this point. Tack the lower corner diagonally opposite the upper corner that you tacked first. Now check to see that the window is square and operates smoothly, and that operable sashes are sitting evenly in their openings.

Tack the other two corners. Shim the unit if further shimming is recommended. Be very

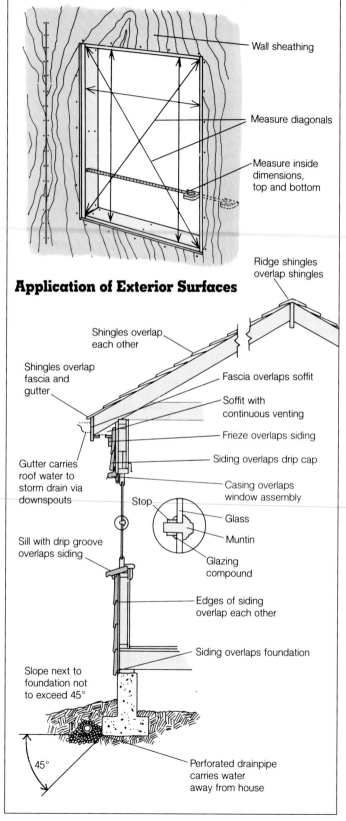

Measure Opening, Including Diagonals

- Wall sheathing
- Measure diagonals
- Measure inside dimensions, top and bottom

Application of Exterior Surfaces

- Ridge shingles overlap shingles
- Shingles overlap each other
- Shingles overlap fascia and gutter
- Fascia overlaps soffit
- Soffit with continuous venting
- Frieze overlaps siding
- Siding overlaps drip cap
- Gutter carries roof water to storm drain via downspouts
- Casing overlaps window assembly
- Stop
- Glass
- Muntin
- Glazing compound
- Sill with drip groove overlaps siding
- Edges of siding overlap each other
- Siding overlaps foundation
- Slope next to foundation not to exceed 45°
- 45°
- Perforated drainpipe carries water away from house

Installing a Window

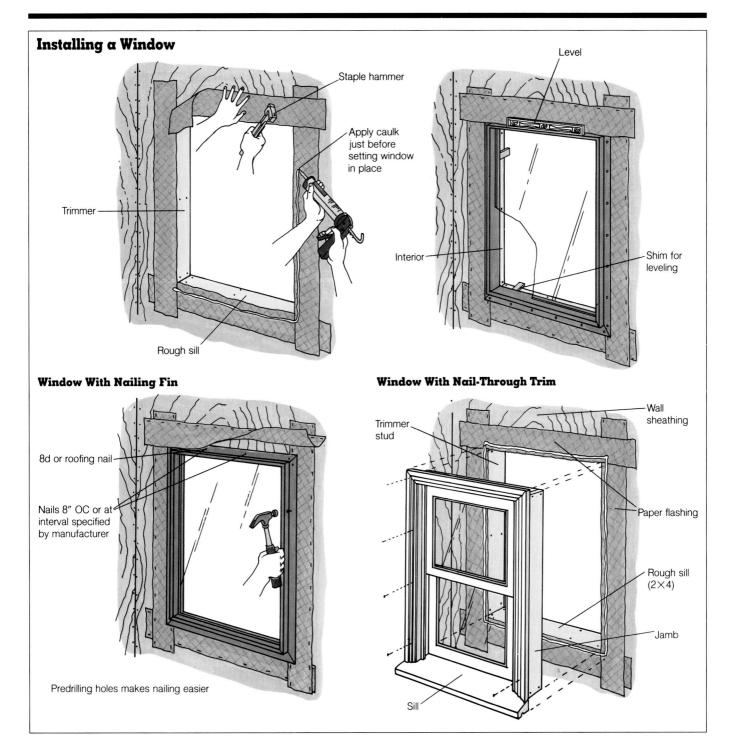

Staple hammer

Apply caulk just before setting window in place

Trimmer

Rough sill

Level

Interior

Shim for leveling

Window With Nailing Fin

8d or roofing nail

Nails 8" OC or at interval specified by manufacturer

Predrilling holes makes nailing easier

Window With Nail-Through Trim

Trimmer stud

Wall sheathing

Paper flashing

Rough sill (2×4)

Jamb

Sill

careful. Too little shimming may allow parts of the unit to sag; too much may bow the jambs. Either way the window may stick or jam. When you're sure that everything is properly adjusted, drive all the nails

home. Refer back to page 34 to make certain that you have papered and flashed the window properly. Caulk around the exterior after the siding is installed. Remember to insulate

the spaces around the window, following the manufacturer's recommendations.

Unlike doors, windows usually come with all of the necessary hardware, including locks. Sometimes this is designed

especially for the unit in question, and it may not be easy to substitute something else. In other cases, the hardware may be replaced with a design of your choosing. It all depends on how it is installed.

Installing a Bay Window

A bay window can be installed in two ways: by simply inserting it into a standard window opening or by altering the wall beneath it to create a bay. The latter method involves more construction, but it opens up the room significantly, and a small seating area can be installed in the alcove.

Bay windows can be purchased ready-made in standard sizes, custom-made to your specifications, or in a kit that you assemble. Unless the window fits tightly against a soffit under overhanging eaves, a roof must also be installed. If you are buying a ready-made unit or a kit, check with the dealer to find out whether the unit includes a precut roof. If it doesn't, you must build one separately.

Installing a Bay Window in a Window Opening

A bay window, whether it is wood framed or metal framed, is installed in much the same way as a standard window. It is, of course, heavier and larger, so have two or three helpers on hand. If the opening must be altered to fit the window, follow the instructions on page 56.

Bay windows are designed to fit either against the existing siding or against the wall sheathing. Be sure to follow the specifications that come with the window when you prepare the exterior of the house to accommodate it.

Knee Braces

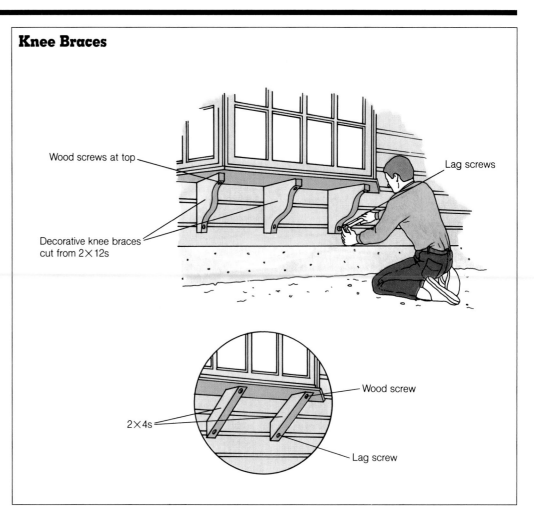

Wood screws at top

Lag screws

Decorative knee braces cut from 2×12s

2×4s

Wood screw

Lag screw

Once the opening is ready, have the helpers set the window into it from the outside and hold it there. From the inside, place a carpenter's level on the stool (the windowsill) and use shingle shims to level it. When the window is level, nail the stool to the rough sill through the shims.

Use the level to check for plumb on both sides of the window. Use shims to make any adjustments and to achieve a snug fit. On wood-framed windows nail the sides through any shims to the trimmer studs on either side. On metal-framed windows nail the flanges to the exterior of the house.

Finally, shim between the headboard and the header to achieve a snug fit and then nail.

The bay window may have to be supported underneath with knee braces. The instructions that come with the unit will specify whether these are needed. If they are, and if the manufacturer did not supply them, make the knee braces as shown from 2 by 4s or from decoratively cut 2 by 12s. Attach them to the house with lag screws sunk into studs. Fasten the top of the knee brace to the bottom of the frame with wood screws. Metal-framed bay windows of this style generally do not need braces.

Installing a Precut Roof

To install a precut roof, first tack the wooden drip cap around the top of the bay window. Fit the front and sides of the roof together on top of the window and mark the outline of the roof where it fits against the house siding. Set the blade on a circular saw to the depth of the siding and cut along the lines. Remove the siding. Fit the roof together against the side of the house and mark the outline on the felt paper that wraps the house. (If there is none, cover the opening with 15-pound felt cut to fit. Staple it to the studs.) Measure the thickness of the plywood roofing and snap new chalk lines that distance inside the outline of the roof. The end rafters, hip rafters, and common rafters will be installed so that the top edges fall along these inner lines.

Before you install the rafters, provide some additional support by tying the top of the window to the house with plumber's tape. This is perforated metal strapping, sold in rolls at hardware stores. Using wood screws with a washer, attach the metal tape to the edge of the frame and to a stud.

The next step is to nail the rafters in place, starting with the two hip rafters. These must be beveled along the top outer edge so that the side pieces of the roof will fit smoothly against the front piece. Use a jack plane to make the bevel if it has not already been done.

When the rafters are installed, lay in a length of insulation over the top of the window with the foil face down. Put the roof in place and nail it to the rafters. Nail metal drip edges around the base of the roof. Then cover it with 15-pound felt. Overlap the hips and staple.

Cover the roof to match the existing roof.

The roof must be flashed where it joins the side of the house. Step flashing is used where the roof slopes down on each side, and a single length of strip flashing is used across the top. The same method is used for all types of roofs—tile, composition shingle, shake, or wood shingle.

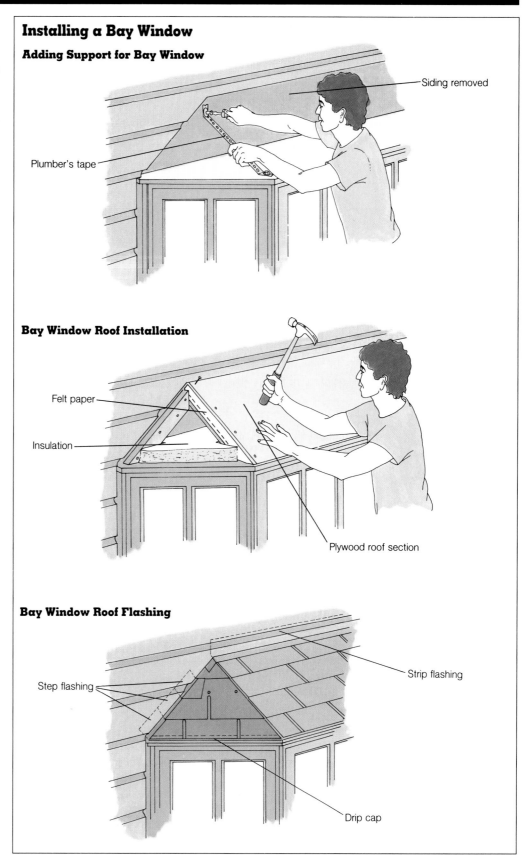

Installing a Bay Window

Adding Support for Bay Window

Siding removed

Plumber's tape

Bay Window Roof Installation

Felt paper

Insulation

Plywood roof section

Bay Window Roof Flashing

Step flashing

Strip flashing

Drip cap

Step flashing is cut from aluminum strips 10 inches long and as wide as the exposure of the shingles. (The exposure is the distance from the base of one shingle to the base of the one above.) This is usually 5 inches for wood and composition shingles and 7 inches for shakes. Have the flashing made up at a local sheet-metal shop.

Note in the illustration on page 63 how the first piece of flashing is slipped up under the siding and then covered by the doubled first row of shingles. The second piece of flashing is slipped under the siding and spaced the distance of the shingle exposure; it is then covered by the second row of shingles. Continue up both sides in this manner. Next, apply the hip shingles. For more details on applying roofing, see Ortho's book *Roofs & Sidings*.

The final step is applying the strip flashing across the top. Cut a length of flashing 6 to 8 inches wide and as long as the roof plus 3-inch ears on each end as shown on page 63. Bend it lengthwise in the middle and slip one part under the siding. Coat the top of the last row of shingles with roofing cement and press the flashing into it. Coat the underside of the strip-flashing ears with cement and bend them over the hip shingles. Finally, run a thick bead of caulk along the gap between the siding and the shingles.

Building an Alcove Support
Alcove Support With Parallel Joists

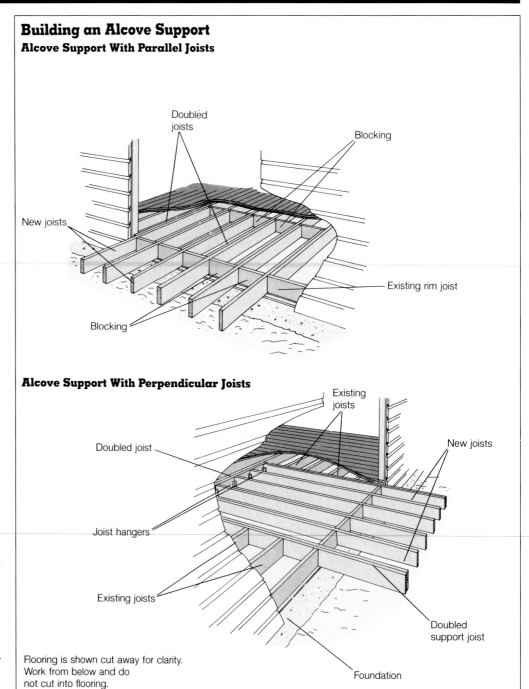

Doubled joists

Blocking

New joists

Blocking

Existing rim joist

Alcove Support With Perpendicular Joists

Existing joists

Doubled joist

New joists

Joist hangers

Existing joists

Doubled support joist

Foundation

Flooring is shown cut away for clarity. Work from below and do not cut into flooring.

Creating a Bay Window Alcove

Altering an exterior wall to create an alcove that conforms to the bay window is more complex than simply installing a bay window in an opening. However, the effort will prove worthwhile. The alcove gives a new dimension to the room. It can provide a snug hideaway for reading or it can become a seating area for a breakfast nook.

The alcove is supported by cantilevered joists the same size as the existing ones that extend over the foundation wall to create a floating effect. Before you begin any construction, go under the house and determine which way the floor joists run. Depending on the direction, use the appropriate tie-in method described below.

Finishing an Alcove Support

Supporting Perpendicular Joists Before Cutting

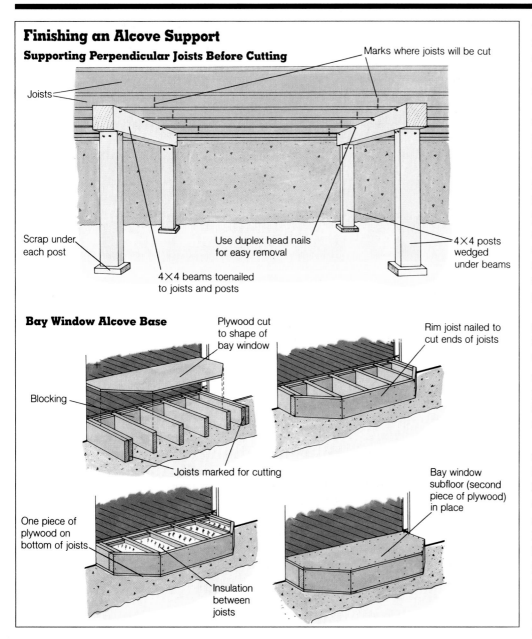

Marks where joists will be cut

Joists

Scrap under each post

Use duplex head nails for easy removal

4×4 beams toenailed to joists and posts

4×4 posts wedged under beams

Bay Window Alcove Base

Plywood cut to shape of bay window

Rim joist nailed to cut ends of joists

Blocking

Joists marked for cutting

Bay window subfloor (second piece of plywood) in place

One piece of plywood on bottom of joists

Insulation between joists

Supporting on Parallel Joists

If the joists on the house run parallel to the joists that will support the alcove, the job is easier. The support joists will simply be nailed to the existing ones.

Measure the height and width of the bay window opening and mark it out on the interior wall to be removed. Remove the interior wall and frame the rough opening as you would for a door (see page 18).

From inside, drive nails through the exterior siding at each corner. Then snap chalk lines from nail to nail to mark the opening on the outside wall.

Remove the siding along the bottom of the opening to expose the floor joists. These will be secured in one of two ways: with a rim joist that extends the length of the building and covers their ends or with blocks placed between their ends. In the first case, cut through the rim joist flush with the edge of the last floor joist on each side of the opening and pry out that section of rim joist. It is nailed to the ends of the floor joists. In the second case, the blocks are toenailed to the sides of the floor joists. Cut in the middle of each block to be removed, pry out the pieces, and pull any nails remaining in the joists.

Measure the total depth of the bay window. Cut the support joists three times that length. If, for instance, the bay window extends 24 inches, cut the support joists 72 inches long. Hammer the support joists into position beside the existing ones, with one third of the length extending out from the house and the other two thirds nailed to the existing joists.

Supporting on Perpendicular Joists

When the floor joists run at right angles to the alcove support joists, sections of several floor joists must be removed to make room for the alcove joists.

The support joists will reach under the floor at least twice the depth of the alcove overhang. Thus, if the bay window extends out 2 feet, you must remove sections of floor joist at least 4 feet back under the house. Determine how many joists must be cut. The next full-length joist will support those in the alcove. It must be reinforced with a joist long enough to be supported on each end by the foundation wall or a girder. Wedge the reinforcing joist in place on the backside of the existing joist. Then nail it to the existing joist.

The existing floor joists must be supported on both sides of the planned opening before any cutting begins under the house. Beneath the joists to be cut, place the supports 2 feet back from the planned opening on each side. Build the temporary support system as shown on page 64, with 4 by 4 beams wedged tightly in place and toenailed together. Toenail the beams to the floor joists.

You are now ready to cut the support joists. Make the cuts on each side 3 inches wider than the actual opening. This allows room for the doubled joists on each side of the opening. Snap chalk lines along the bottoms of the joists to be cut. Make the cuts with a saber saw or a reciprocal saw and finish up with a handsaw. The rim joist along the foundation wall will have to be drilled first so that a saw blade can be inserted. When the cuts are complete, pry the joists loose from the subfloor. Use nippers to cut the nails flush.

The alcove support joists should be spaced the same as the existing floor joists, which is usually 16 inches on center. Support them on the reinforced joist with joist hangers. To install them, first place one support joist at each side of the opening and nail it to the ends of the cut floor joists. Facenail a second joist to the first one to make a double joist. Space and hang the intervening joists. Remove the support system. Now you can start framing the alcove.

Framing the Alcove

To make the alcove subfloor, place the bay window on a sheet of ¾-inch exterior plywood and mark the outline of the window frame on it. Cut the plywood on the outline. Then use it as a pattern to cut another one.

Place one of the pieces of plywood on top of the alcove studs, align it in the opening and against the existing subfloor, and trace its outline on top of the joists. Remove the plywood, place a straight length of 2-by lumber on the *inside* of the lines, and mark. Cut the joists on this inside mark. This will allow room for the rim joist to be nailed to the ends of the support joists and still be flush with the edge of the plywood.

Cut the ends of the rim joist material (which should be of the same stock as the support joists) at an angle matching the bay window (usually 45 degrees). This will ensure a smooth fit. Nail the rim joist to the ends of the support joists.

Nail one piece of plywood to the bottom of the support joists, place insulation between them, and install the subfloor.

Now lay out and construct the kneewall (also called the cripple wall) around the perimeter of the alcove in the manner described on pages 18 to 25. Cut the plates where the sidewalls join the front walls at angles matching the window. Put the front wall in position first. Then nail the two sidewalls to it and to the trimmer studs in the rough opening.

Finally, insert the bay window in the opening as described on page 62. Trim out the interior and install a seat across the alcove to complete the job. For more helpful ideas here, see Ortho's books, *Finish Carpentry Basics* and *How to Design & Build Storage Projects*.

A variation of the bay window, this bow window is made up of several casement windows. Bow windows are available as complete manufactured units. For special situations, custom bow windows can be assembled from individual windows of any type or from a combination of types that blends with the architecture of the house.

Installing Glass Block

There are many types of glass block. The commonest patterns distort the image coming through, but clear glass block is also available.

Many home-improvement centers carry glass block. They generally also stock all of the accessories and instructions you'll need in order to install it. Remember that glass block does not provide structural support. You'll have to create an opening for a glass block window just as you do for a regular window or door.

Glass block can be installed with mortar, much like standard brick. If you use this method, be sure to coat all the wood members—particularly the rough sill—with a thick layer of asphalt emulsion and to include an expansion strip around all sides of the opening. Large glass block windows that are installed with mortar need additional reinforcement. Just how much depends on the style of the block. The reinforcement consists of steel rods in the courses of mortar as well as panel anchors that screw into the sides and top of the framing and are embedded in the courses. The space between the edges of the glass block and the window frame should be sealed with caulk, not mortar, to allow for expansion and contraction.

Another method of installation uses mortar combined with plastic connectors, which act as spacers and provide reinforcement between the blocks. The pieces out in the middle area of the window are shaped like plus signs. The ones at the edges are shaped like *T*'s and are screwed to the frame for support. One advantage of this method is that since the blocks rest on the plastic spacers, you don't have to worry about the weight of the blocks squeezing the soft mortar out of the lower joints.

The last method is the mortarless channel technique. A metal channel is installed all around the opening; the blocks fit into it; and special strips are used to maintain the proper horizontal spacing. When all of the blocks are installed, all the joints are filled with silicone caulk. This eliminates the need to mix mortar and also allows you to change your mind and readjust the blocks before they are caulked.

To simplify installation you can special-order preassembled glass block units, which you then install and caulk into place.

If ventilation is needed you can order vent windows that fit glass block. Simply substitute the vent unit for some of the blocks.

Installing Glass Block

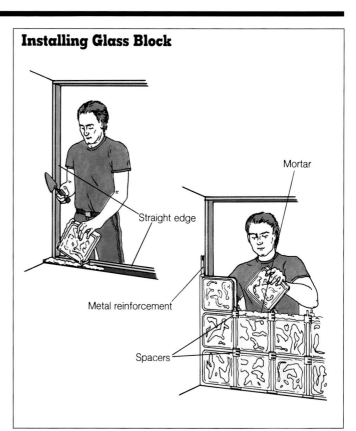

Straight edge

Mortar

Metal reinforcement

Spacers

Glass block is an ideal solution for situations where both light and privacy are needed.

TRIMMING OUT THE WINDOW

There are several options for exterior and interior window trim. At this point it's a good idea to reread the section on trimming out doors (pages 36 to 38).

Exterior Trim

In the old days trim was functional as well as decorative; it served to keep the weather out of the joint between the window and the siding. Some of today's windows don't need trim for protection. Aluminum, vinyl, clad, and pretrimmed windows can all be completed with siding alone. Traditional windows were often finished with a wide trim, so sometimes wide trim is installed around modern windows to achieve that traditional look. It's really a question of individual taste. Windows with nailing fins tend to look more contemporary when they are left untrimmed. If you'd like a more old-fashioned look, consider a wide trim board. Windows that come with preinstalled wood can sometimes be ordered with special trim that measures 1 by 4 or 1 by 6. If you are adding exterior trim to a window with nailing fins, you may have to make a very small channel in the back of the trim piece to get it to clear the nailing fins and lie flat against the wall.

You'll also need to decide, if you add trim to the outside, whether to trim the four sides of the window identically, like a picture frame, or to install a stool and an apron (the horizontal piece right under the stool). The latter will give a more traditional look, but the picture frame trim is more appropriate on some styles of houses.

Measuring for Exterior Trim

The placement of exterior window trim, also known as casing, is best determined with a steel tape measure. For windows with sills that protrude from the building and extend beyond the bottom of the side casings, measure the side casings first. Touch the tip of the

These stately custom-made windows are ideal candidates for formal trim. The side units are double-hung, with divided panes in each sash. The heights of the panes are matched to those of the divided panes in the center Gothic window. The head trim of the side windows coordinates with the crown molding at the top of the walls.

Measuring for Window Trim

Horizontal Board Siding Wall Finish   Stucco or Shingle Wall Finish   Windows Without Sills

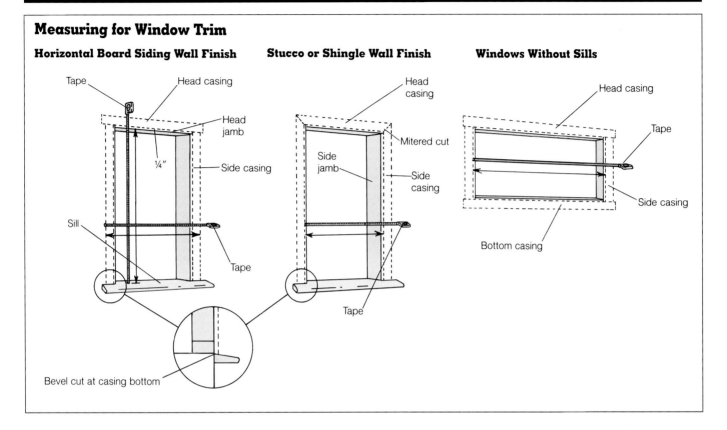

tape measure to the windowsill and extend the tape vertically along the side jamb to just past the point where it intersects with the head jamb. Mark the cut line ¼ inch past the intersection. This allows for a ¼-inch reveal, or setback, from the edge of the jamb when the casing is installed. Once the side casings are cut and tacked in place, determine the length of the head casing by measuring the distance between the outside edges of the side casings. The usual practice is to add ½ inch to this dimension, to allow the head casing to extend ¼ inch beyond each side casing. See illustration on page 37.

The casings should be beveled on the bottom. If they are being installed over wood siding, they should be square on the top. If the trim is being installed with stucco or shingle siding, the side and head casings are usually mitered where they intersect. In this case, the measurement for the head casing is taken between the inside edges of the side casings, and the miter is cut from that dimension.

Other types of window frames require different procedures. Should a bottom casing be necessary on a window without a sill, its length is determined by measuring between the inside edges of the side jambs of the window and then adding ½ inch for reveal,

plus twice the width of the side casing, plus ½ inch for overhang. Tack this piece in position, allowing ¼ inch of bottom-jamb reveal. Then determine the lengths of the side casings by measuring from the top edge of the bottom casing to ¼ inch past the bottom edge of the head jamb. Once these side casings are tacked in position, the head casing can be measured, cut, and installed as described for trimming windows with sills.

Metal windows with nailing flanges should be installed before the wallcovering. The casing may or may not be

required. With shingle the casing is optional; if you elect to use it, it should be installed before the wallcovering. With horizontal and vertical board siding and plywood, the casing is installed. With stucco, brick, and stone, no casing is used. The casing for wood-framed windows is installed before or after the wallcovering, depending on what type of wallcovering is used. With shingle, stucco, brick, and stone, the casing is usually installed first. With horizontal or vertical board siding, the casing can be installed first or last. With plywood siding the casing is usually installed last. If your house

Installing Square-Cut Window Trim

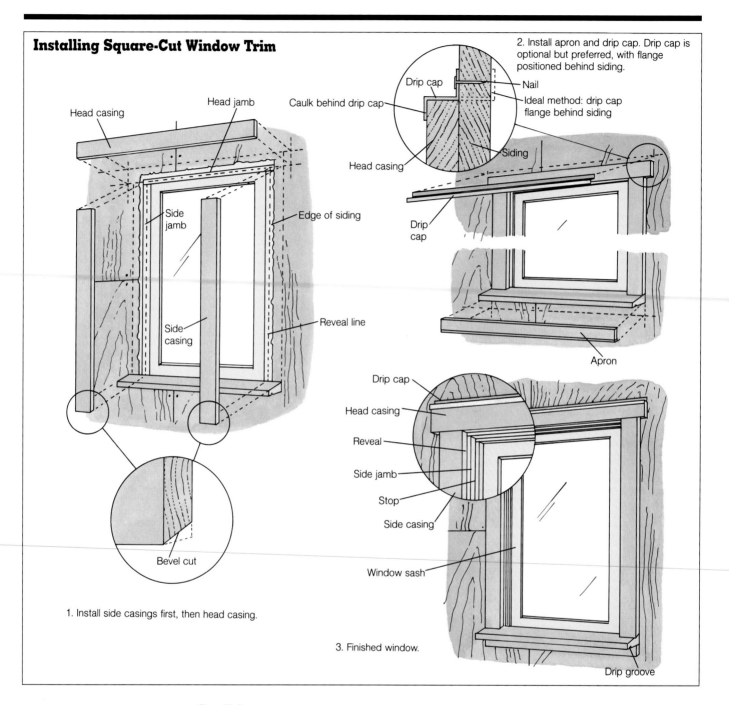

Head casing

Head jamb

Side jamb

Side casing

Edge of siding

Reveal line

Bevel cut

1. Install side casings first, then head casing.

2. Install apron and drip cap. Drip cap is optional but preferred, with flange positioned behind siding.

Drip cap

Caulk behind drip cap

Head casing

Nail

Ideal method: drip cap flange behind siding

Siding

Drip cap

Apron

Drip cap

Head casing

Reveal

Side jamb

Stop

Side casing

Window sash

3. Finished window.

Drip groove

is of a unique design that calls for unusual windows, wall-coverings, or casing procedures, ask a knowledgeable source to help you to determine whether, and when, to install casing.

Caulking

If the casings are to be painted, small gaps or cracks can be caulked first. Casings that are to be stained or sealed with a clear material must fit together well, because most caulks will show through and be unsightly. (A limited range of colored caulks is available. One of these may match the stained or sealed wood.)

Nailing

Hot-dipped galvanized common and box nails are most often used for exterior applications. Both are weather resistant and hold well. Finishing nails are not usually used on exteriors; their holding capability is inferior to that of common and box nails.

Use stainless steel nails if a clear finish is to be used or if the nailheads will be exposed.

Installing Mitered-Cut Window Trim

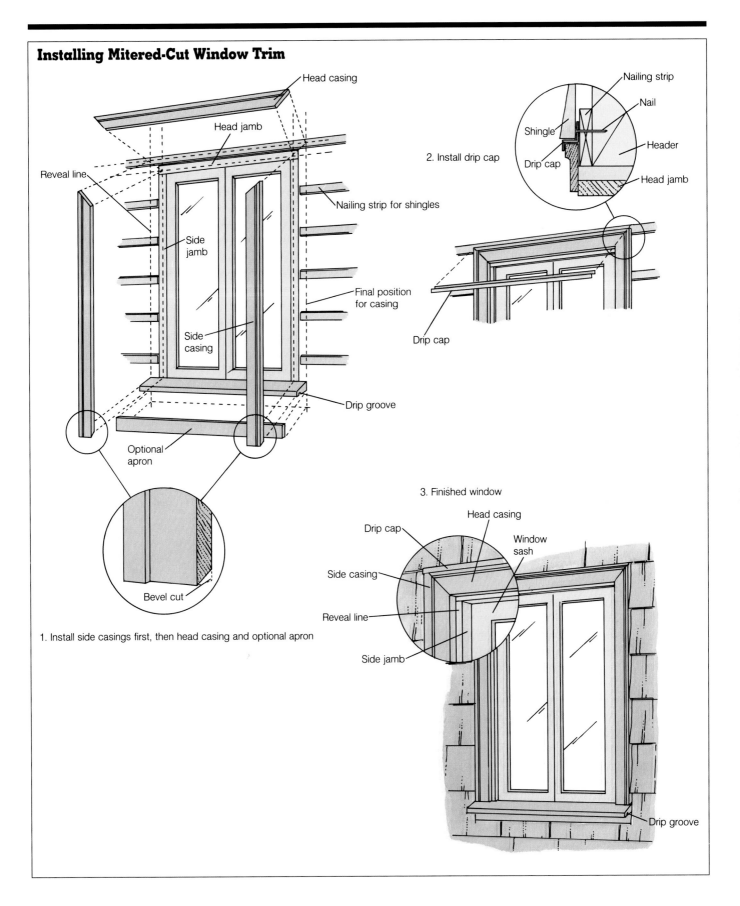

Head casing

Head jamb

Reveal line

Side jamb

Side casing

Reveal line

Nailing strip for shingles

Final position for casing

Drip groove

Optional apron

Bevel cut

1. Install side casings first, then head casing and optional apron

2. Install drip cap

Nailing strip

Nail

Shingle

Header

Drip cap

Head jamb

Drip cap

3. Finished window

Drip cap

Head casing

Window sash

Side casing

Reveal line

Side jamb

Drip groove

Installing Trim on Metal-Framed Sliding Windows

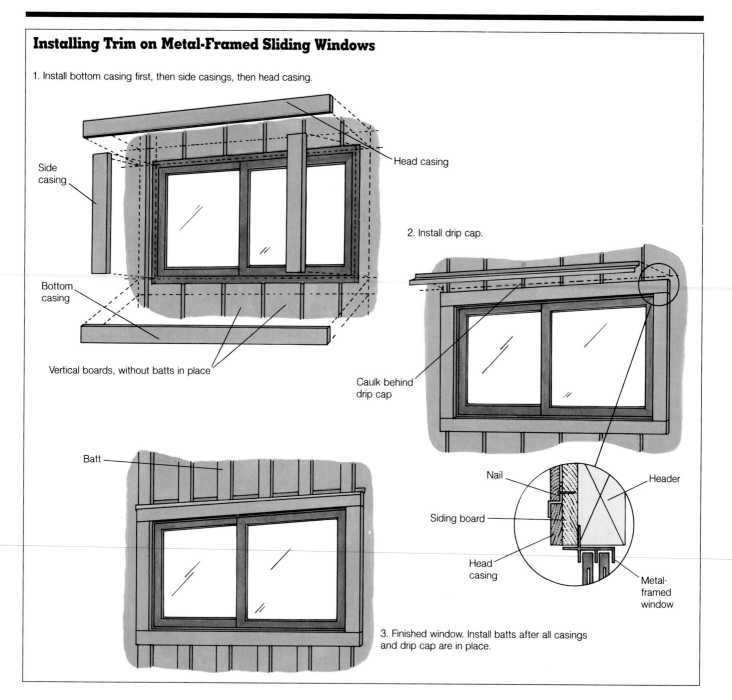

1. Install bottom casing first, then side casings, then head casing.

Head casing

Side casing

2. Install drip cap.

Bottom casing

Caulk behind drip cap

Vertical boards, without batts in place

Batt

Nail

Header

Siding board

Head casing

Metal-framed window

3. Finished window. Install batts after all casings and drip cap are in place.

As a rule, nails should be evenly spaced between 12 inches and 18 inches apart. The top and bottom nails should be about 1 inch from the ends of the casing. Closer nailing may be necessary where the stock is bowed or otherwise irregular.

Interior Trim

The traditional interior window trim included a stool, an apron, and casing around the two sides and the top. This is still a popular way to finish an interior window, although windows can also be trimmed out picture-frame style.

Although walls are generally of a stock thickness, this is not always so, particularly when the house is old or has been remodeled. Manufacturers build their windows in such a way that special pieces must be fitted to the inside jambs, bringing them out flush with the surface of the walls, so that the casings can be applied. You may have to make these special pieces (which are called jamb extensions) yourself. Some manufacturers will provide extensions if you furnish

Interior Trim Options

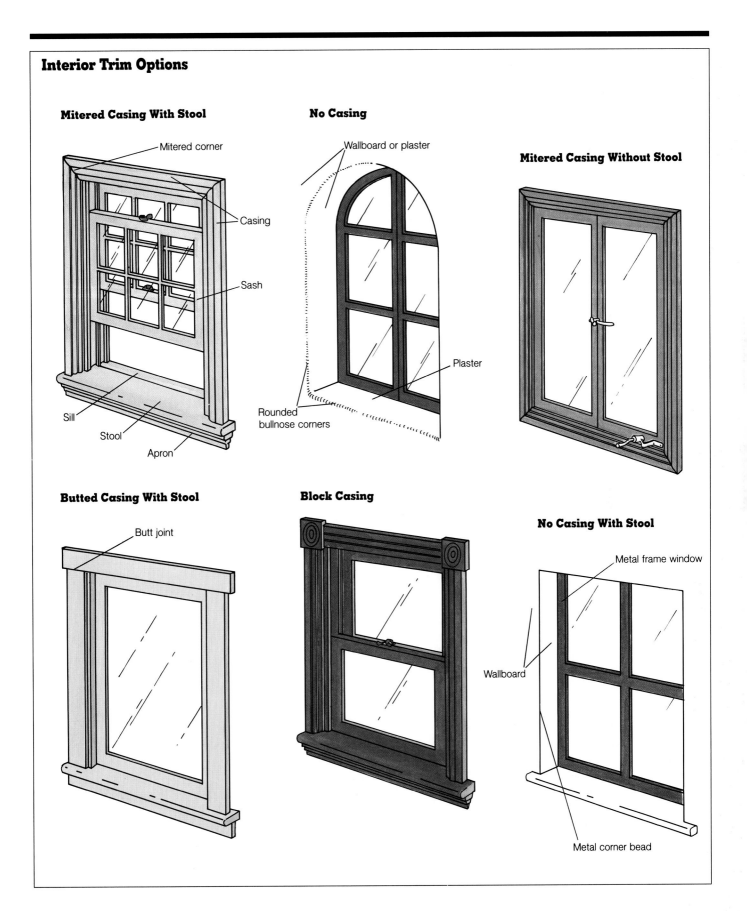

Mitered Casing With Stool

Mitered corner

Casing

Sash

Sill

Stool

Apron

No Casing

Wallboard or plaster

Plaster

Rounded bullnose corners

Mitered Casing Without Stool

Butted Casing With Stool

Butt joint

Block Casing

No Casing With Stool

Metal frame window

Wallboard

Metal corner bead

them with the overall thickness of the wall.

You can trim out the side jambs of metal and vinyl windows entirely in wood, but more often these windows are installed with wallboard returns on the top and side jambs and a wood stool and apron. This is an attractive and functional arrangement. Some people use wallboard stools, but these do not wear very well and can't be recommended.

Before you start, check for flaws and correct them. Look for jambs that protrude beyond the plane of the wallcovering. These make it nearly impossible to get good joints. Look too for jambs that don't quite meet the surface of the finish wall. If a jamb protrudes, planing it will usually solve the problem. In the latter case, it may be necessary to install jamb extensions to bring the surfaces even, or to plane the wallboard. Look for jambs that are bowed or curved. This flaw is usually corrected by straightening the jamb as the trim is nailed.

Finally, remember to use finishing nails appropriate to the thickness of the casing. For example, for the most common casing—pine beveled—which is between 1⅝ inches and 2¼ inches wide and is ⅜ inch thick at the jamb side and ⅝ inch thick at the trimmer side, use 3d finishing nails at the jamb side and 6d finishing nails at the trimmer side. For the more traditional straight casing (usually Douglas fir), which is 3½ inches wide and ¾ inch thick, use 6d finishing nails at the jamb side and 8d finishing nails at the trimmer side.

Sizing and Positioning Window Trim

Determining Head Casing Length

Head casing length equals distance between side casings

Marking the Reveal

A combination square is used to mark reveal

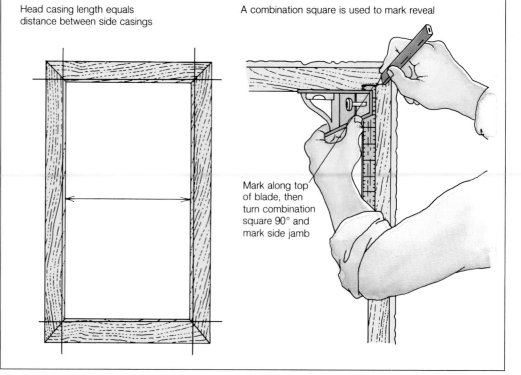

Mark along top of blade, then turn combination square 90° and mark side jamb

Blocked casing gives these windows a traditional look. The vertical trim pieces extend full-length to integrate the fixed units above with the casement windows below.

Interior Window Casings

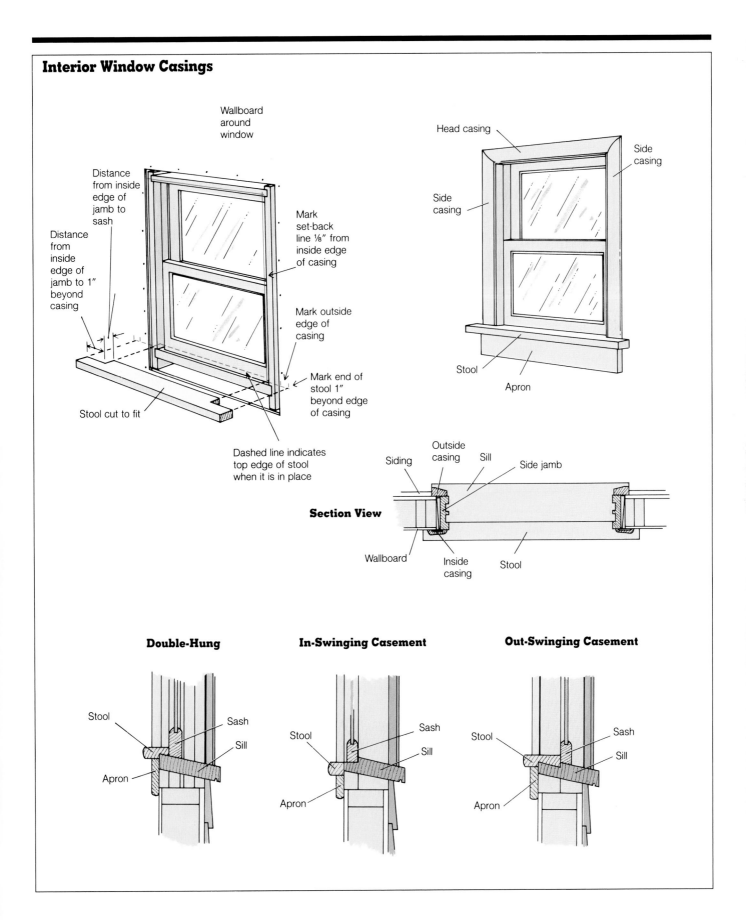

Wallboard around window

Distance from inside edge of jamb to sash

Distance from inside edge of jamb to 1" beyond casing

Mark set-back line ⅛" from inside edge of casing

Mark outside edge of casing

Mark end of stool 1" beyond edge of casing

Stool cut to fit

Dashed line indicates top edge of stool when it is in place

Head casing

Side casing

Side casing

Stool

Apron

Section View

Siding

Outside casing

Sill

Side jamb

Wallboard

Inside casing

Stool

Double-Hung

Stool

Sash

Sill

Apron

In-Swinging Casement

Stool

Sash

Sill

Apron

Out-Swinging Casement

Stool

Sash

Sill

Apron

SKYLIGHTS

Today's skylights range from the simple plastic bubble all the way up to large units replete with such features as electrically driven openers and shading devices. Modern improvements ensure that a well-installed skylight will not only look good but also be trouble free. You can use skylights for brightening a space, balancing light, and bringing in ventilation. They're particularly well adapted to improving attics and when used in groupings can become the architectural focus of a room or of the entire home.

An example of successful planning, these skylights illuminate the room with dramatic beams of light.

DESIGN AND PLANNING

Designing and planning skylights requires close attention to practical as well as aesthetic considerations. Heat, light, ventilation, and access for operation and maintenance should all be taken into account.

Selecting the Style

There are two basic styles of skylights: the conventional type and the more recently developed roof window. Before you choose a style, you will need to decide whether you want fixed or venting units. Fixed units do not open, as their name implies. Most venting skylights do open, but some incorporate a flap that provides ventilation. Venting skylights are also referred to as operable skylights.

Conventional Skylights

Use these in places where view and operation don't depend on being at eye level with the skylight, or on being able to walk right up to the unit to operate it. As their name suggests, skylights are usually installed in overhead locations.

Many skylights are available with wood frames, which harmonize better with the styles of some homes than does aluminum. Aluminum is also widely used for skylight frames, however, and today there is a much wider choice of colors than there was in the past, providing more flexibility in matching the new skylights to the look of the existing house.

Skylights come with either flat glass or plastic; the latter is often available in a bubble shape as well. The flat-glass units generally blend in better with a traditional-style house;

the bubble types are more at home in contemporary designs. Diffusing glass (which is actually a plastic) is available in bubble and flat designs. Some of the bubbles have interesting geometric shapes that enhance the light-diffusing characteristics of the unit.

Roof Windows

One concept that influences skylight planning today is that of the relatively new so-called roof window. Roof windows are skylights designed to be installed at eye level. They require a roof with a fairly steep pitch, and they are especially effective at transforming attic space into usable rooms. Roof windows function much like a conventional window, particularly in that they afford a view straight out and can easily be operated to provide ventilation. The glass panel pivots in such a way that both sides are easily cleaned from inside the room. Roof windows usually have wood frames, clad on the outside, and flat glass.

Choosing the Location

When it comes to locating a skylight, you may not have much choice, but if you do, consider the light you'll be letting in. On a roof slope facing south or west, the skylight will admit a lot of direct summer

sun. That can increase room temperature and fade rugs and furniture. Placing the unit on an east or north slope will give you just as much light but less direct sunshine. If you must place a skylight where it will receive a lot of direct sun, there are several ways to control the amount of light that enters the room.

Consider access too. A skylight must be placed so that you can reach it for cleaning without endangering yourself. If the skylight is operable, the controls should be within easy reach.

Heat and Ventilation

To prevent excessive heat build-up, consider operable or venting skylights. These units, installed high in the house, can

cool the interior considerably by allowing hot air to escape.

Skylights can also provide solar heating, especially in greenhouse installations. However, you can take advantage of the sun in the main house too. For instance, if you want skylights to help heat the house in winter but keep it cool in summer, the answer might be a clear, low-E, argon-filled glazing, which lets the sun's rays in during the winter while keeping the heat from escaping. This can be combined with an awning or blind system that can be kept closed during the hot summer months.

Consider the slant at which the skylight will be installed. Sunlight strikes the earth's surface at a low angle during the

The casement windows in this installation can be opened for ventilation, allowing the use of fixed bubble skylights.

winter and at a high angle during the summer. For this reason, a skylight or roof window that is nearly vertical will receive more direct sunlight in the winter, when heat gain is desirable, and less in the summer, when it is not.

Light

Small skylights on the north side of a roof may not need shades, but large skylights, or those exposed to very bright sun, will benefit from some form of light control.

Many skylight and roof window manufacturers offer exterior and interior awnings or blinds that are specifically designed to work with their products. These provide total control over the entry of light. However, they do require minor maintenance.

If there is a ceiling below the roof where you want to install a skylight, you will need to construct a light well. This provides another way to control the quality of light entering the room. Light wells with straight shafts are easier to build than flared ones, but flaring the shaft will provide better light distribution and a more attractive appearance.

Glazings are also used for light and UV light control. Most of the glazing features discussed in the second chapter (page 54) are available for skylights, including bronze- and gray-tinted glass, low-E reflective coatings, and gas-filled double-pane glazing. Plastic skylights are available in bronze tints, and also in white tints, which are good at diffusing light. Better still, some manufacturers offer plastic

glazing made of a honeycomb material especially designed to diffuse light evenly. The dead-air spaces in the honeycomb provide good insulation.

Whether or not to use tinted or semitransparent glazing is partly an aesthetic decision. People often do not want to sacrifice the dramatic look of clear glazing, particularly when the unit affords a special view. Ease of cleaning should also be considered. Skylights that are not clear may need cleaning less frequently than clear ones, because they have less of a tendency to show dirt.

Access

Venting and operable skylights that are too high to reach by hand can be opened with an extension handle, generally incorporating a crank. The same is true for roof windows. Some manufacturers offer the option of a remote-controlled electric motor. A further option with motor drives is a battery-powered backup system for times when the electricity is interrupted. This is a handy thing to have if your skylights are open when the power goes off and it starts to rain.

Because roof windows can be rotated into the room for cleaning, they may be a good choice if the roof is inaccessible or dangerously steep. It is often easier and safer to clean such a window from a stepladder inside the room than from outside on the roof.

Security and Safety

If you use skylights or roof windows to convert an attic into a usable room, keep in

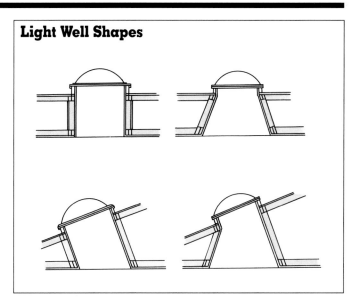

Light Well Shapes

mind that the building code will require you to provide a minimum-sized window opening as an emergency exit if the room is ever to be used for sleeping. It's a good idea to provide such an exit in any case. As a rule, the exit window must be at least 24 inches high by 20 inches wide, with the sill not more than 44 inches off the floor. Check the local building code, however, to make sure that you have the most up-to-date information. Codes are constantly being revised. It's heartbreaking to be asked to remove and replace skylights because they don't satisfy the latest code requirement.

The local code may also specify what types of glazing are permissible in skylights. Laminated safety glass, tempered glass, or some combination of the two is generally required. There may also be some restrictions on plastic glazings, though these rarely apply to single-family houses. Finally, if you want to install a skylight on a part of the roof

that is close to a property line, check to see whether any code restrictions apply. As was explained on page 9, these restrictions are meant to help prevent the rapid spread of fire from house to house.

Where to Shop for Skylights

Skylights are sold in many of the same places as doors and windows, and they are purchased under the same conditions (see pages 10 and 11).

Showrooms may have mock-ups of skylights mounted on sloping ceilings. Showrooms are particularly helpful if you are shopping for operable units, since they make it easy to see whether the unit operates smoothly and is well finished.

There are also shops that specialize in custom-made aluminum-framed skylights. You can deal direct with many of them, and they can fabricate skylights to almost any shape you wish. This is expensive, naturally, but it may be worthwhile if you need a unit in an unusual shape or size.

SELECTING FLASHINGS

At the time you purchase a skylight, you should also plan the flashing materials. Some skylights come with an integrated flashing and installation package. However, many skylights do not. It is important to know what type of flashing you will need as soon as possible in case you will have to order special items.

Be sure that whatever flashings you use are appropriate for your particular roofing material. Flashings for heavy roofs, such as tile or shake, differ somewhat from those used on composition or wood shingle, but the same installation principles generally apply to both types.

If the unit you buy doesn't include flashings, you can have them made up at any sheet-metal shop. This is a common procedure, and if you aren't sure what kind of flashing you need, the sheet-metal fabricator can help you to decide. The technique of flashing a skylight curb is discussed on page 85.

All skylight flashings have two parts in common. These are the saddle flashings, which cover the top and bottom of the skylight curb and also wrap partway around the sides. The upper piece is called the head flashing, and the lower piece is called the base or tail flashing.

For most types of shingle roofing, step flashings are used on the sides of the curbs. For flat roofs, tar-and-gravel roofs, and those covered with roll roofing, a continuous L-shaped side flashing is used. This goes under the head flashing and over the base flashing.

Roofing materials that have irregular shapes or thicknesses, such as tile, heavy shake, or metal, require special flashings. Head flashings for these high-profile roofing materials are the same as those used for shingle roofs. The flashing slips under the roofing material and so is not affected by the extra thickness. Base flashings, however, lie on top of the roofing. They must therefore be made to conform to it closely, in order to keep out wind and water. This is usually done by using a corrugated soft-lead flashing, which can easily be worked by hand to conform to the contours of the roof. Lead works particularly well with tile. Use conventional or lead flashings with shake roofs, depending on how thick and irregular the shakes are, and on how much the skylight is exposed to wind. Metal roofing comes in many patterns, and it is best to follow the recommendations of the manufacturer for skylight flashings. Tile and metal roofs usually require a continuous side flashing.

Roof window manufacturers sometimes use a U-shaped side flashing. The roofing rests on one leg of the U and the other leg runs up the side of the skylight. Water is carried away in the channel of the U, and a good seal between the roofing and the corresponding leg of the U is promoted by the use of a thick soft-foam gasket. A similar U-shaped side flashing can be fabricated to use on a conventional skylight with a tile roof, or with shakes, if they are thick enough to call for it. With metal roofing, follow the flashing recommendations of the manufacturer.

It is very important to use the correct kind of side flashing. Never use an L-shaped flashing on a shingle roof. Step flashings are interwoven with the shingles, so water that gets into the corner where the step flashings turn up the curb makes its way to the top surface of the next shingle as it works its way down the roof. If water gets into the joint between an L-shaped flashing and the roof, there is nothing to direct it back out, so it will leak into the house.

Whichever type of flashing you use, you will need to tell the sheet-metal fabricator how high the sides of the curb are and also how thick the roofing is. The top edge of the flashing should come to just below the top of the curb, so that the lip of the skylight will overlap the flashing. If you are retrofitting a skylight to an existing roof, subtract the thickness of the roofing material from the height of the curb, so that the flashing doesn't project up too high.

Be sure to use compatible nails with metal flashings. With copper flashings, for example, use only copper nails. Nails and flashings of incompatible metals will develop galvanic corrosion, which will quickly eat away the nails or the flashing or both.

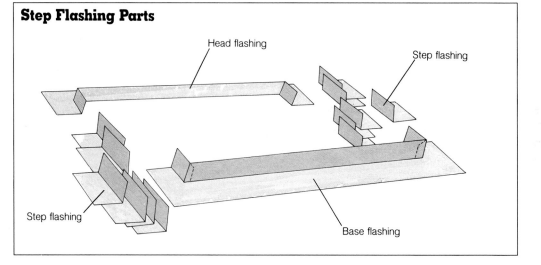

Step Flashing Parts

Head flashing

Step flashing

Step flashing

Base flashing

Top left: An array of venting skylights allows excess moisture to escape from the spa room below. Top right: This venting skylight mounted in a composition shingle roof uses step flashings and a flat apron. An added feature is the semitransparent pull-down awning, which reduces heat gain without blocking the view. Bottom: Skylights and roof windows can be used in combinations to fit different architectural styles.

INSTALLING THE SKYLIGHT

It is not difficult to install a skylight, but the job must be done correctly and safely. This section discusses ways to frame the opening, install the skylight, and do a weather-tight job of flashing.

Safety Precautions

Start by reviewing the rules of safety. First and foremost, you don't want yourself or any helpers taking a fall off the roof. Wear shoes with a good grip and use safety lines and scaffolding at the eave if necessary. Another unfortunate way to wind up on the ground floor is by falling through the ceiling as you work on the skylight opening or on the light well. Keep your feet on the ceiling joists when you are working in the attic space. You may find it helpful to place some boards or scraps of plywood across the ceiling joists temporarily to give yourself a place to stand. Finally, cutting roof shingles

and decking throws a tremendous amount of noxious dust around. Besides safety glasses and hearing protection, be sure that everyone wears a dust mask. This is especially important if you have a helper

working in the attic while you are cutting from above.

Weather

Bear the weather in mind when tackling a skylight installation. Usually you can finish the job in a day. If you have good access from below, you may be able to do all the framing before you cut into the roof at all. In case of rain have a tarp on hand that is long enough to reach a few feet over the roof

ridge from the top of the skylight, and a few feet to each side and below the opening. Use a tarp with grommets, so that you can tie boards or other weights to the edges to hold it in place. Don't try to hold down a tarp with loose boards or bricks—they may tumble off the roof. In a windy situation you can also run a rope from one of the grommets into the skylight opening, in case the wind should start to blow really hard.

Skylight Curb

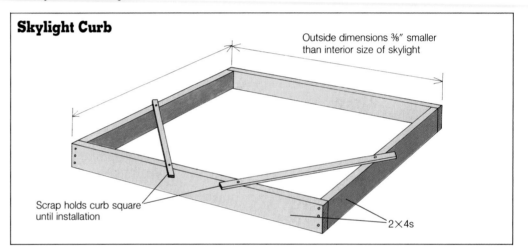

Outside dimensions ⅜" smaller than interior size of skylight

Scrap holds curb square until installation

2×4s

Skylight Framing Patterns

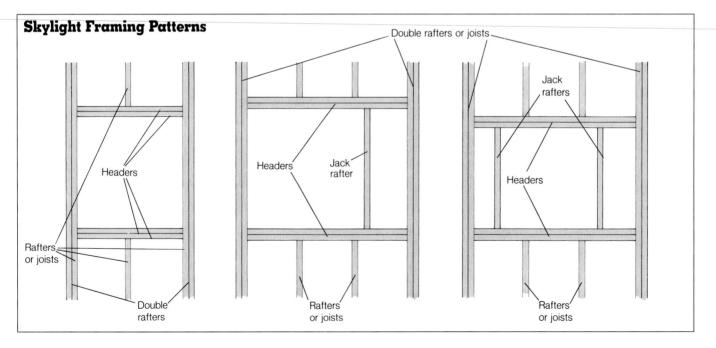

Double rafters or joists

Headers

Rafters or joists

Double rafters

Headers

Jack rafter

Rafters or joists

Jack rafters

Headers

Rafters or joists

Installation Procedures

This section discusses the procedures for installing a conventional skylight, using flashings that are fabricated separately from the unit. Roof windows come with all the necessary parts and very clear step-by-step instructions. Installation of roof windows varies with the manufacturer, and the only way to ensure a proper installation is to follow precisely the directions that come with the unit.

Constructing the Curb

Start by building a curb on the roof for the skylight to rest on. The flashings that you had fabricated will run up this curb. Make sure that the curb is about ¼ inch smaller than the head and base flashings, so that they can be slipped easily into place.

The curb is made from 2 by 4 lumber as illustrated on page 82. Measure and cut carefully so that it is ⅜ inch smaller all around than the interior dimensions of the skylight. This gap allows the skylight to fit over both the curb and its step flashing.

When the curb is nailed together, square it with a framing square. Then tack two light pieces of wood across the diagonal corners to hold it in shape.

Making the Opening

A skylight is normally positioned in the roof so that it and its light well will be centered in the ceiling of the room below. If there is no ceiling, and thus no light well, half of your construction problems are eliminated. If there is a ceiling,

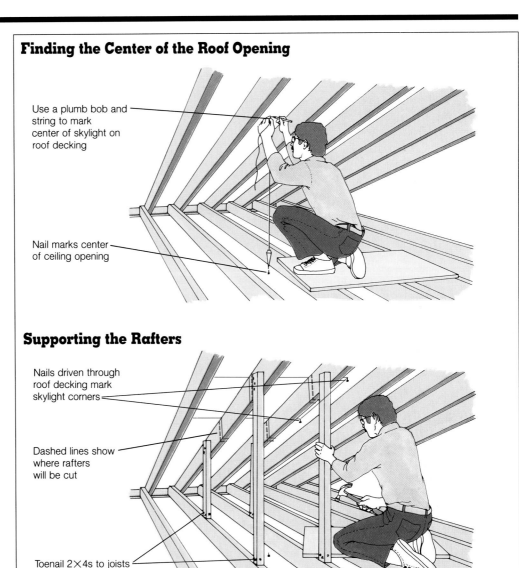

Finding the Center of the Roof Opening

Use a plumb bob and string to mark center of skylight on roof decking

Nail marks center of ceiling opening

Supporting the Rafters

Nails driven through roof decking mark skylight corners

Dashed lines show where rafters will be cut

Toenail 2×4s to joists

decide where you want the center point of the light well to be and drive a nail through the ceiling there. In the attic, drop a plumb bob from the underside of the roof deck to the point of the nail in the ceiling to find the center of the roof opening. If necessary, move this point a few inches to eliminate unnecessary cutting of rafters or joists. Try to line up one side of the skylight on an existing rafter.

The illustrations on page 82 show the different patterns of

framing an opening. Choose the way that best meets your particular needs. The simplest way is to use existing rafters rather than building in one or more jack rafters.

Once you have found the center point of the roof deck, mark the inside dimensions of the curb across the rafters and the underside of the roof deck. Do this with a framing square, taking careful measurements. At each corner mark, drive a nail to protrude above the roof.

Now measure down 3 inches below the bottom line of the curb outline (toward the eaves) and 3 inches above it (toward the ridge). Snap straight chalk lines across the bottoms of the rafters at these marks. The additional 3 inches above and below allows for the double headers that will be installed between the rafters. The intervening rafters will be cut on these lines.

Before you cut, support the rafters by nailing 2 by 4s to

them above and below the marks, with the bottoms of the supports resting on ceiling joists and toenailed in place. The opening in the roof can be cut now, or you can wait until you've finished the interior framing. When you do cut it, you might want to have a friend stationed below to help you handle the cutout piece.

When you're ready to cut the opening in the roof, snap chalk lines to connect all the nail points. The inside corners of the curb will be at the points where the nails came through the roof. The outside edge of the curb will be 1½ inches outside the nails. To give yourself a little room to work, snap another chalk line 2 inches outside the first one. Set the blade of a circular saw to the depth of the roofing shingles and then cut them along this line.

Remove the shingles. Snap new lines on the roof deck, using the nail holes as guides. Set the blade on the saw to ⅛ inch more than the thickness of the roof deck and cut along the lines. Remove the decking.

Back inside the attic, cut any rafter that crosses the opening you made on the chalk line 3 inches above and below the outline of the curb. Measure the distance at the top and bottom between the two uncut rafters nearest the sides of the opening. Cut four header boards of this length from the same size stock as the rafters. At the top or bottom of the opening, fit a header board between the two existing uncut rafters. Nail through the rafters into the ends of the header with 16-penny (16d) nails. Nail the middle section of the header to the end of the cut

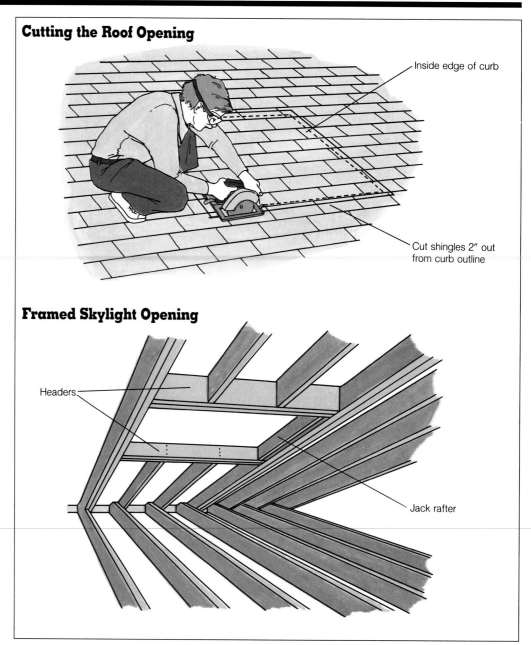

Cutting the Roof Opening

Inside edge of curb

Cut shingles 2" out from curb outline

Framed Skylight Opening

Headers

Jack rafter

rafter. Do the same at the other end of the opening. Now nail each second header in place over the first one in the same manner. Install jack rafters as needed. The roof opening is now framed. Remove the braces.

If you planned a light well that is angled or splayed, cut the rafters at the corresponding angle before you install the headers.

Installing a Curb-Mounted Skylight

Set the curb over the opening; double-check to ensure that it is centered and square; then toenail it from the inside through the roof and deck into the rafters and headers. Install the flashing (see page 85). Apply a bead of caulk or some cushioned weather stripping to the top of the skylight curb. Then drop the skylight over the curb and flashing. Nail it to the curb along the upper edge or through the factory-drilled holes. Cover each nail head with a dab of caulk or roofing cement.

Installing the Curb

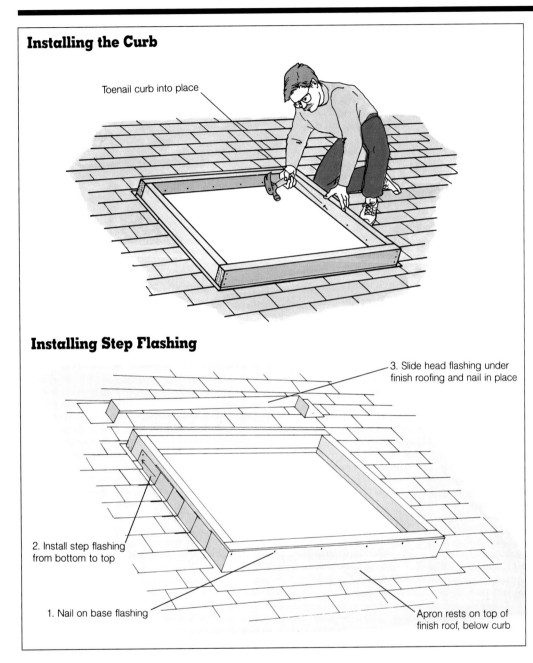

Toenail curb into place

Installing Step Flashing

3. Slide head flashing under finish roofing and nail in place

2. Install step flashing from bottom to top

1. Nail on base flashing

Apron rests on top of finish roof, below curb

Flashing a Skylight Curb

Before you install the flashing, review the principles outlined on page 34. Remember that proper overlap is the key to making flashing work. A properly flashed skylight should need no tar or caulk to be waterproof. This is not, however, to say that tar and caulk have

no place in skylight installation. In a very windy location, they will help to prevent water from being blown up into the small joints between flashings. They can also be used under the base flashing to keep water and air from blowing up between it and the roofing. The illustration shows that the uppermost edges of the base

flashing go beneath the lowest pieces of step flashing. As you work your way up the side of the skylight curb, each step flashing overlaps the one below it and slips under the adjacent shingle. The sides of the head flashing overlap the highest pieces of step flashing, and the top edge of the head flashing must be completely under the roofing.

If you are installing a skylight in an existing roof, you will need to lift shingles away from the roof in order to install the flashing. Work carefully to avoid breaking them, since broken shingles can cause leaks. Composition shingles break easily in cold weather. If you must work on a cold day, try warming the shingle with a heat gun or a blow dryer to soften it before you try to lift it. The shingle may also be stuck to the one below it. Shingles come with an adhesive that makes them stick together to improve their wind resistance. To free them, use a flat prybar, sometimes called a wonder bar. A flexible putty knife will also do.

To begin the installation, first fit the base flashing in a bed of caulk around the bottom edge of the curb. Note that the apron rests *on top* of the shingles along the bottom edge of the curb. This directs water over the shingles and off the roof. Don't place the apron beneath the shingles. This will direct water under the shingles and cause a leak.

Nail the base flashing to the curb along the top edge of the flashing. Place the nails so that they will be covered by the skylight.

Fit the first piece of step flashing overlapping the base flashing. Slide it beneath the shingle, embedding the edge next to the curb in caulk. Nail it to the curb along the top edge.

You may also need to nail the step flashing to the roof in order to make it lie flat. Don't do this if it isn't necessary; the fewer holes in the roof, the better. If you do need to nail

Setting the Curb-Mounted Skylight in Place

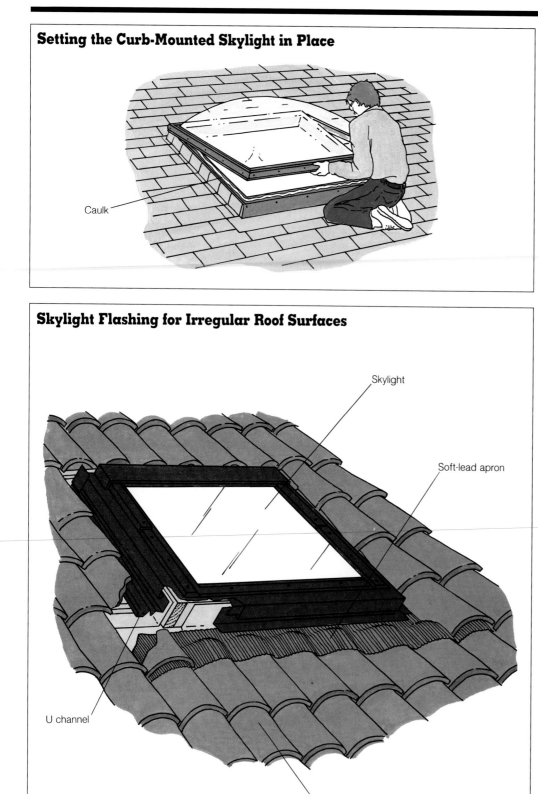

Caulk

Skylight Flashing for Irregular Roof Surfaces

Skylight

Soft-lead apron

U channel

Roofing material (tile shown; this type of flashing
also works with materials such as heavy shakes)

the step flashing to the roof, gently lift up a shingle and nail the flashing so that the shingle will cover the nail. If you can't take a swing at the nail because the shingle is still in the way, here's a little trick: Hold a heavy wonder bar or a piece of metal bar stock on the nail head. Then, using your hammer, strike the bar just below the edge of the shingle. That should drive the nail, leaving the shingle undamaged.

Continue installing the side flashings on both sides until you reach the top.

Fit the head flashing around the top of the curb. Its apron must fit completely under the shingles. A common mistake is to get the edge under just one row of shingles, visible through the small gaps between the sides of the shingles. Those gaps will let water under the head flashing, producing a leak. Avoid the temptation to fill the gaps with caulk. It's best to get the flashing up the rest of the way. The usual difficulty is in removing the shingle nails without destroying the shingles. Use a wonder bar with a slight curve and a prying notch in the long end. Slip the bar up under a shingle, catch the nail with the notch, and pry it out.

If there are holes or broken shingles when the job is done, patch them with caulk or roofing cement.

In the so-called self-flashing units, the flashing is incorporated into the skylight itself. These units are more prone to leaks than conventional skylights and are best installed by professional roofers. They are also very difficult to use with thick roofing materials. However, don't discount them entirely if you are looking for a very low-profile skylight. Because they don't have a separate flashing, they do hug the roof. Just be very careful to have them installed properly.

Constructing the Light Well

Now that the skylight is in place, you can open the ceiling and finish the light well without fear of rain.

The first step is to frame the ceiling opening, which can be done before you cut the ceiling. First, support the ceiling joists. Do this by laying two 2 by 4s flat across the joists 2 feet back from the planned opening. They should reach two rafters beyond the last rafter on each side that must be cut. Drill holes through the 2 by 4s and into the top of each joist; then fasten them with 4-inch screws.

To frame the ceiling opening, follow the same procedure that was used to frame the skylight opening.

Once the framing is complete, cut out the ceiling opening by punching a wallboard saw through the ceiling from above and cutting along the edge of the framing material.

The light well is constructed with 2 by 4s, spaced not more than 24 inches apart on center. The tops of the 2 by 4s are toenailed to the rafters and the bottoms to the joists. If you have installed a wide skylight, with jack rafters and jack joists, they will line up directly above and below each other. However, if you have a skylight that is designed to fit between two existing rafters, you will run into a little problem. Note that since ceiling joists are nailed to the sides of rafters where they

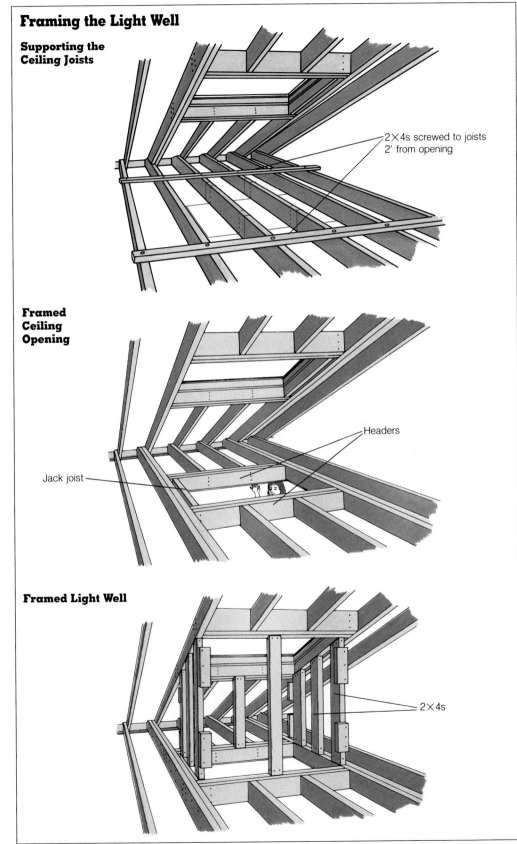

Framing the Light Well

Supporting the Ceiling Joists

2×4s screwed to joists 2' from opening

Framed Ceiling Opening

Headers

Jack joist

Framed Light Well

2×4s

meet on the cap plate of the stud wall, they are not lined up directly under the rafters. To learn how to achieve an uninterrupted surface in the light well, study the illustration on page 87. The 2 by 4s on one side are nailed to the side of a joist and toenailed to the bottom of a rafter. On the other side the 2 by 4s are nailed to the face of the rafter and toenailed to the top of the joist. The framework now falls smoothly from the skylight opening.

One or more angles must be cut at the top and bottom of the 2 by 4s, depending on what angle you chose for the light well. Cut the 2 by 4s a couple of inches less than the measured distance from the roof deck to the ceiling at roughly the desired angle. Place the 2 by 4s against the rafters and joists at the precise angle. Then mark the 2 by 4s where they cross the rafter and joist. Cut along that line. Then toenail the 2 by 4s to either the rafter or the joist, depending on which side of the opening they are on. At each corner nail another 2 by 4 on the back edge of the corner supports to provide a nailing surface for the wallboard.

Staple insulation batts around the light well with the foil facing into the well.

Finish the light well by covering the interior with paneling to match the room or with wallboard painted a light color for good reflection.

This attic living unit features a dormer with three small windows and a skylight with a flared opening. They provide abundant natural light and add drama to the ceiling.

Marking Angles for Light Well Framing

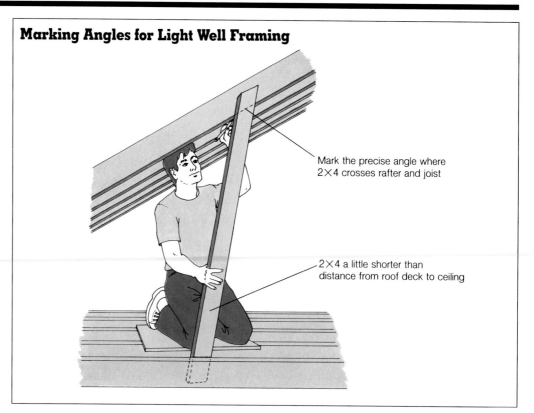

Mark the precise angle where 2×4 crosses rafter and joist

2×4 a little shorter than distance from roof deck to ceiling

TRIMMING OUT THE SKYLIGHT

Skylights can be trimmed out in almost any way you can imagine. A lot depends on whether you want to focus on the skylight itself or on the light that it admits to the room.

If you are trying to draw attention to one area by flooding it with light, use unobtrusive skylight trim. Elaborate trim will emphasize the skylight. If there is a light well, you must decide whether or not you want to trim it out. Usually a light well is just finished off in wallboard or plaster, and the surface is painted a pale color so that light entering the well is reflected into the room. Most skylights are designed so that the wallboard can be run right up against the bottom edge. In this case, no further trim is required. You may need to shim one or more walls of the well to ensure that the wallboard meets all the edges of the skylight evenly.

An alternative to wallboard or plaster is to line the light well with wood trim. Follow the techniques used for trimming out the side jambs of windows. Finish the job with a flat piece of trim resting on the edge of the side jamb and on the surface of the roof. Alternatively, install a narrow trim band where the wallboard meets the skylight unit.

The wood trim added to these support beams makes them more massive and integrates the skylights into one unit.

MAINTENANCE & REPAIR

Thinking of doors, windows, and skylights as openings in the weatherproofed exterior of the house emphasizes the importance of keeping them well sealed, tight-fitting, and in good working order. Doors, windows, and skylights that look their best and operate efficiently are more pleasant to live with than poorly maintained units. They will also help to lower energy bills and to maintain the investment you have in your home. This chapter describes maintenance and repair techniques that will simplify the task. It also includes a special section on weather-stripping and caulking.

Regular preventive maintenance of doors, windows, and skylights will help to keep small problems from becoming large ones.

REPLACING GLASS AND REPAIRING SCREENS

Two of the most common window problems— broken glass and damaged or deteriorated screens—are easily solved with the simple repair techniques described here.

Replacing Broken Glass

Broken glass in most types of windows can easily be replaced. Before you start, though, consider whether the window is likely to be broken again. If so, it might be wise to replace the broken pane with acrylic or tempered glass.

If one pane of a double-pane window is broken or cracked or if the seal between the panes has failed (indicated by fogging between the panes), the entire sash must be replaced. For wood-framed sash windows, remove the shards from the sash, wearing gloves to protect yourself.

Next, remove the putty by scraping it with a putty knife. If the putty is too hard, soften it with a soldering iron. Pull out all the glazier's points and then scrape and sand the old wood. Now coat the bare surface with a sealer or linseed oil. This keeps the wood from drawing the oil out of the new putty or glazing compound.

The simplest way to get a new pane of glass is to measure the window opening carefully and ask a glazier to cut a replacement piece for you. Have the new pane cut ⅛ inch smaller in both dimensions than the window opening.

Working from the outside, spread a thin layer—about

⅛ inch—of glazing compound on the edge of the opening. Then insert the new pane. Do not press so hard that you cause the cushion layer of compound to squeeze out around the glass.

Next, still working from the outside, tap the glazier's points in place around the window. Space them about 6 inches apart. Drive them in halfway with a hammer and a screwdriver.

Roll the final layer of glazing compound into a rope about ½ inch thick. Using your fingers, press it into place, covering the glazier's points. Now, using the putty knife, press the rope in farther and leave a smooth, beveled bead, starting at one corner and moving to the next in one continuous stroke. The bead should extend to the outer edge of the sash and should be as high as the sash edge on the inside of the glass.

Clean the glass. When the putty or compound is dry enough to touch without leaving a fingerprint, repaint it. Let the paint lap onto the glass about 1/16 inch as an added seal.

Replacing broken glass in a fixed-pane window requires special materials and professional skills to achieve a weathertight seal. Broken panes in a fixed-pane window should be replaced by a glazier.

Casement windowpanes are replaced in much the same manner as panes in wood-framed sash windows. However, instead of glazier's points, the panes are held with small spring clips inserted into holes in the frame.

After the putty has been completely removed, sand the edges and repaint them to prevent corrosion. Replace the windowpane as outlined above, using the spring clips instead of glazier's points.

Methods of Securing Glass

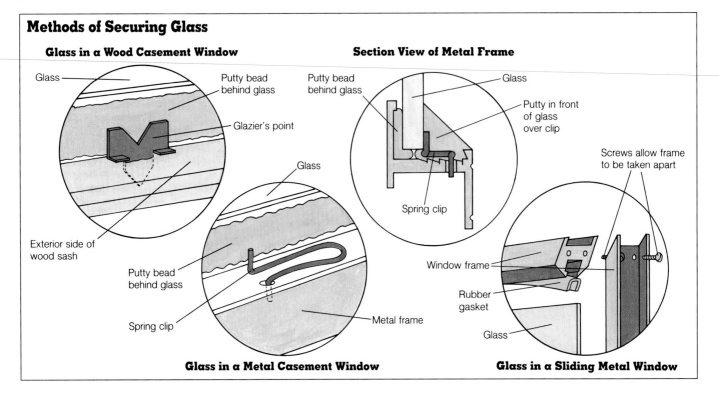

Glass in a Wood Casement Window

Glass

Putty bead behind glass

Glazier's point

Exterior side of wood sash

Section View of Metal Frame

Putty bead behind glass

Glass

Putty in front of glass over clip

Spring clip

Glass

Putty bead behind glass

Spring clip

Metal frame

Glass in a Metal Casement Window

Screws allow frame to be taken apart

Window frame

Rubber gasket

Glass

Glass in a Sliding Metal Window

Some casement windows have metal strips to hold the panes in place. Make sure that the rubber gasket has not been damaged. If it has, replace it.

To remove broken glass from aluminum sliding windows, the sash must be taken apart, usually by removing screws. The glass is held in place by a rubber gasket. Pull this out and remove all the particles of glass. Then reinstall the glass and gasket and reassemble the sash.

For a storm window with a wood frame, replace the glass as described for a wood-framed sash window. If it has a metal frame, refer to the instructions for aluminum-framed sliding windows.

To replace broken glass in a door, see the appropriate window section above, depending on what the framing material is. For sliding glass doors consult a glass-and-window supply firm.

Repairing Damaged Screening

What appears to be a small hole is sometimes actually just the screen wires spread apart. Use a nail or an awl to realign them.

For small tears in wire screens, either buy a ready-made patch or make your own from matching screening. To make your own patch, cut a square of screen about twice the size of the hole and then unravel all four sides a little. Bend these individual wires at a right angle, push the patch over the hole, and bend the wires back.

The method used for wire screens won't work for plastic.

If the hole is very small, align the broken ends and bond them with epoxy resin. If it is a larger tear, overlay it slightly with a matching piece of screen and glue this in place with epoxy resin. Align the individual strands for a smooth job.

Replacing Screening

Torn or deteriorated screen can be replaced with new material, available at hardware stores and home-improvement centers.

If the frame is made of wood, first pry up the molding that holds the screen in place. Work slowly so that you don't split it. Remove the screening and the staples.

Cut the new screen 1 inch larger than the opening. Staple the bottom edge in place. Now stretch the screen, using either of the methods illustrated here. Staple the top while the screen is stretched. Then release the tension and do the sides. Trim the edges with a utility knife and replace the molding.

If the frame is made of aluminum, use a screwdriver to pry up one corner of the metal or plastic spline that holds the screen in its channel. Work your way around the door. Cut the new screen 1 inch larger than the opening. Then press it into the channels, using the special roller tool designed for this purpose, which is available at hardware stores. Replace the spline as you work your way around the door. The combined pressure of the tool and the spline will pull the screen tight. Trim off the excess, using either tin snips or a utility knife.

Repairing Screens

Fixing a Hole in Wire Screening

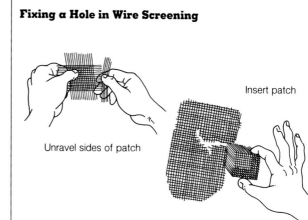

Unravel sides of patch

Insert patch

Stretching Screening on a Wood Frame

Method 1, Using Clamps and Boards

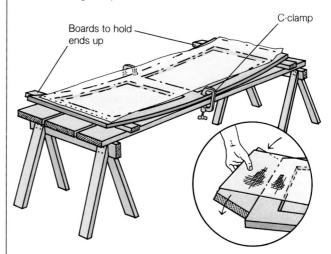

Boards to hold ends up

C-clamp

Method 2, Using a Board to Stretch Screening

Replacing Screening in an Aluminum Door

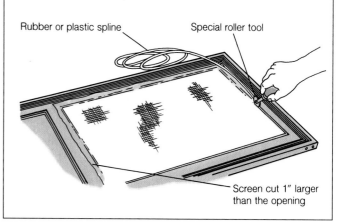

Rubber or plastic spline

Special roller tool

Screen cut 1" larger than the opening

SOLVING DOOR PROBLEMS

You can get used to living with a door that doesn't work right, because it seems like such a lot of trouble to fix it. However, fixing such doors should be high on your priority list. The misalignment can seriously damage both the door and the jamb, and a misaligned door causes drafts.

Fixing a Door That Sticks

Doors may stick for several reasons. Dampness may cause a wood door to swell; the hinges may be worn out of adjustment; or the door may simply need minor trimming. The wrong repair can create more problems than it solves, so inspect the door carefully before you repair it.

Coping With Swollen Wood

A wood door may not quite fit during a wet or humid period because moisture makes it swell. If you plane it down to fit during the wet weather, however, it will often be loose during the dry season, when it shrinks back to normal. You will have to judge whether it sticks badly enough to justify that. If it just binds slightly, soaping the area will probably help. The real solution to swollen wood is to take the door down, strip off all the paint, seal it properly, and stain or paint it again.

Fixing Hinges

If the door tends to stick year around, the first area to investigate is the hinges. Open the door and check to make sure that all the screws are tight. If one or more are loose and won't tighten down, the wood behind has been stripped by the screw threads. An easy and effective solution is to remove the screw, coat a wood match with glue, and push into the hole. When it is dry it will provide ample filler to reset the screw.

If the door sticks and the hinges are all tight, stand back and study the closed door. If it is hanging crooked, the gap on the latch side will be uneven. Wherever the gap is wider—at the top or at the bottom—shim that hinge out to straighten the door. Loosen the leaf of the hinge on the jamb, cut a piece of cardboard the height of the butt hinge and about ¼ inch wide, slip it behind the leaf, and retighten the screws.

Shimming entails some trial and error. This can be eliminated by correcting the hinge in another way. Remove the pin and shim between the door and the threshold until the door is straight in the jamb. Now take a large wrench or

Repairing Hinges

Shimming a Hinge

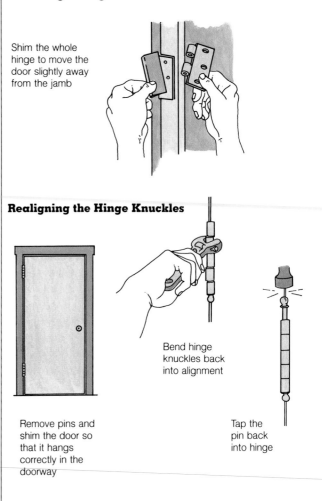

Shim the whole hinge to move the door slightly away from the jamb

Realigning the Hinge Knuckles

Remove pins and shim the door so that it hangs correctly in the doorway

Bend hinge knuckles back into alignment

Tap the pin back into hinge

Adding a Thrust Bearing

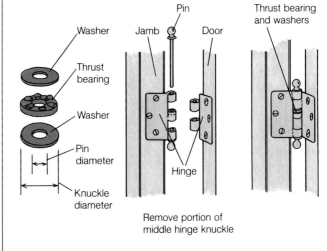

Washer

Jamb

Pin

Door

Thrust bearing and washers

Thrust bearing

Washer

Pin diameter

Knuckle diameter

Hinge

Remove portion of middle hinge knuckle

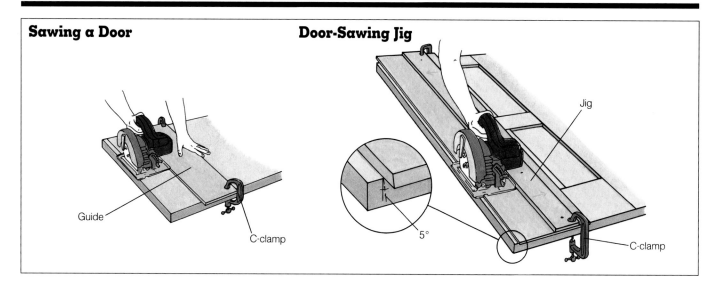

Sawing a Door

Guide

C-clamp

Door-Sawing Jig

Jig

5°

C-clamp

---

a pair of smooth-jawed pliers and bend the knuckles of the hinge leaf attached to the jamb until they are aligned with those on the door. Reinsert the pin. You should be able to realign the door about ⅛ inch without binding any other hinges.

Butt hinges on heavy exterior doors eventually wear, causing the door to sag. A careful look at the hinges will tell you whether this is the problem. If it is, or if you are installing a big custom-made door, use this tip: Add a thrust bearing, available at bearing supply stores, to the center hinge. Thrust bearings, which come in a variety of sizes, have a series of hardened rollers built into them. Use a bearing washer on each side of the bearing and install as illustrated on page 94, in place of a portion of the middle knuckle on the jamb leaf. (Cut the knuckle away with a hacksaw.)

Sanding, Planing, and Cutting

A wood door that sticks can often be fixed with just a little sanding or planing. Sanding is slower but more accurate when only a little wood must be removed. Wrap the sandpaper around a block of wood to keep it flat on the edge of the door. Remember that whenever a door is sanded, planed, or cut, it must be resealed and stained or painted.

The first problem is to find just where the door sticks. If you aren't sure, slip a piece of paper in the closed door around the suspect area. Wherever the paper can't be pulled out, the door is binding.

To work on the door, remove it from its hinges, bottom hinge first. If you don't have a helper or a door buck (see page 33) to hold the door, you can put one end in a corner of the room to brace it. When planing the edges of a door, always work with the grain, or you will gouge the wood. When planing the top or bottom of a door, work from the outer edges toward the center. If you

plane from the center to the edge, you will certainly split a large chunk out of the stile. When you have finished planing, lay a straightedge on the door and sight along it for irregularities. These may be corrected by sanding.

When a door must be cut to fit an opening or to clear a new threshold, there are three key points to keep in mind. The cut must be perfectly straight; you must not leave a ragged saw edge; and hollow-core doors cannot be trimmed more than 1 inch.

Cutting freehand with a circular saw is too inaccurate when you are working on a door. First, draw a line where you want the cut. Then clamp a straight board on the door to guide the saw. The factory edge of a piece of plywood is good for this. Position the saw carefully on the line at one end and clamp the guide into position. Measure from the line to the guide and set the far end of the guide at the same distance.

For smooth cuts use a carbide-tipped plywood saw blade. Even this fine-toothed

blade will not prevent hollow-core veneer doors from splintering. They must first be scored with a utility knife on the cut line. Carry the line clear around the door and then score it, using a straightedge guide. This severs the surface fibers, producing a smooth edge when the door is cut.

If you have many doors to do, the saw jig illustrated here will be a great time saver. Make the jig out of a piece of ¼-inch hardboard or plywood. It should be about 7 feet long and 12 inches wide. Cut a perfectly straight piece of hardboard or plywood to the same length and 2 inches wide. Glue and screw it down the center of the first piece. Use a square to double-check that the saw blade is set at a 90-degree angle. Set the saw against the guide and cut down one side of the jig. Set the saw at a 5-degree angle, which is the amount exterior doors are trimmed on the inner edge to clear the jamb, and cut down the other side. Mark each side clearly. To cut any door just clamp the jig along the line and, using it as a guide, run the saw along the edge.

Repairing Doors

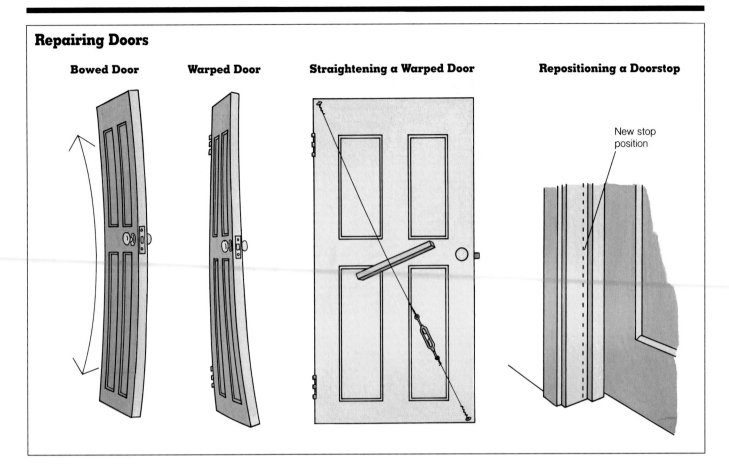

Bowed Door **Warped Door** **Straightening a Warped Door** **Repositioning a Doorstop**

New stop position

Fixing a Warped Door

Warping or bowing can render a good door nearly useless. Rather than throwing it away, try straightening it.

If the door is simply bowed in the middle, you may be able to straighten it with weights. Set it on a pair of sawhorses or chairs, with the bulge up. Then place heavy objects—books or bricks or whatever—in the center until the weight straightens the door.

If the door is twisted, it must be pulled back into line. This is done with a couple of lengths of wire and a turn-buckle, available at hardware stores. First, put two screw hooks at the diagonal corners of the warp. Attach the wires to

the screw hooks and the turn-buckle. Then tighten. Set a short length of 2 by 4 on edge in the center with the wire stretched over it to provide more lever-age. Increase the tension daily over a period of three or four days. Tightening all at once may pull the screw hooks out. Once the door is straight, re-move the screw hooks and fill the holes with putty.

When a door is just slightly out of line and you don't want to try to straighten it, you may be able simply to move the doorstops to conform with the door. Tap a flat trowel down the edge of the stop on both sides. If it is not set into, or part of, the jamb, you'll be able to pry it loose gently. Close the

door, move the stop to the proper position, and nail. That twisted door should now look quite respectable.

Replacing a Threshold

Most thresholds are made of hardwood and will take years of wear. Eventually, however, they will show their age and need to be replaced.

First, inspect the threshold. Is it flush against the door-jambs, or does it extend under them? In the first case, removal is simple. Just take off the door-stops and then pry up the thres-hold with a crowbar.

Generally, however, the threshold extends under the jambs. In this case, saw

through the threshold on each side of the jambs next to the stops, which can be left in place. Pry up the center piece and use a hammer and chisel to knock out the end pieces under the jambs. Do as little damage as possible to the pieces, so that you can use them as a pattern for cutting the new threshold. If the old threshold was too badly damaged to use, measure the opening carefully and cut a cardboard pattern to fit.

When tapping the new threshold into place, use a ham-mer with a protective block of wood. Don't force the threshold, or you may split the jamb. In-stead, plane or sand the edges that fit under the jamb. If one end is low, shim it with strips of felt paper. Once you have a good fit, remove the threshold and lay three thick beads of caulk on the subfloor to seal out drafts.

Since hardwood splits easily, predrill the nail holes. Make them about half the diameter of the nails. Better yet, predrill the threshold to accept countersunk screws. Tighten the screws and fill the holes with wood putty.

Fixing a Hole in a Hollow-Core Door

Hollow-core doors are easily damaged, but fortunately they are also easy to repair.

The first step is to pull away the splintered wood around the break and lightly sand the hole to remove any rough edges. Next, ball up a sheet of newspaper, coat the back of it with glue, and push it into the hole. Use a wide putty knife to cover the paper with a layer of patching compound. This is a powder that is mixed with water to make a fast-setting repair material for holes in such places as floors and walls. Let the first coat dry overnight and then apply the second coat, bringing it out flush with the surface of the door. If you try to fill the hole with just one thick layer, it will shrink too much as it dries. When the repair is completely dry, sand it smooth and repaint the entire door.

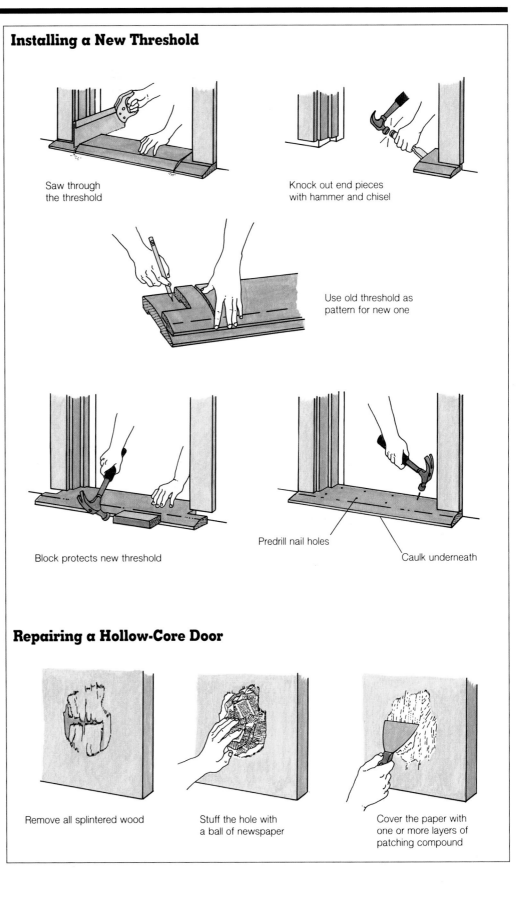

Installing a New Threshold

Saw through the threshold

Knock out end pieces with hammer and chisel

Use old threshold as pattern for new one

Block protects new threshold

Predrill nail holes

Caulk underneath

Repairing a Hollow-Core Door

Remove all splintered wood

Stuff the hole with a ball of newspaper

Cover the paper with one or more layers of patching compound

Fixing a Splintered Door

The bottom or top edge of a wood—particularly a veneer hollow-core—door may become splintered where it fits too tightly in the doorframe.

Remove the door if necessary and then squirt some white glue under the splintered area. Push the veneer in and wipe off the excess glue. Place a piece of waxed paper over the glued area and apply a clamp. Use scrap wood under it to protect the door.

If a piece of wood is missing from the door, fill the hole with wood putty. If the hole is more than ⅛ inch deep, fill it to half its depth, let it dry overnight, and then smooth in a top layer. Sand it when it is dry and paint it or stain it to match the door.

Fixing a Dent in a Metal Door

Although metal doors are durable, they can be dented by a sharp blow. For the best way to repair your particular door, consult with the dealer or the manufacturer.

However, one standard way of fixing dents is to sand the area down to bare metal and then use a putty knife to smooth in the plastic filler that is used to repair dents in car bodies. Small cans are available in any automotive store. Sand the filler smooth when it is dry and paint it to match the door.

Strengthening a Screen Door

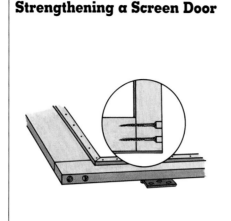

Countersink long wood screws through the stiles into the ends of the rails

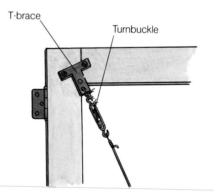

T-brace

Turnbuckle

Run light wire in a figure 8 through turnbuckle

Repairing a Splintered Door

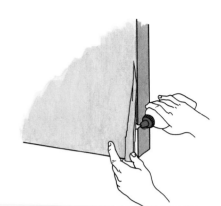

Squirt white glue behind splinter

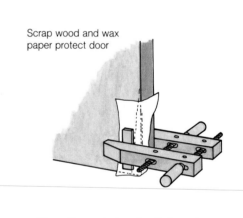

Scrap wood and wax paper protect door

Clamp the crack closed until glue sets

Fixing a Bent Sliding-Door Rail

Once in a while a rail in a sliding glass door gets bent. This is uncommon, but it may happen. If the irregularity is small, bend the rail back into line with a pair of pliers. If the bend is 2 or more inches long, place a block of 2 by 4 against it and hammer the block to bring the rail back into line.

Fixing a Sagging Screen Door

Screen doors often sag because they come apart at the joints. To fix this, pry the joint apart slightly, fill it with glue, and clamp it. Then drill through the stiles into the ends of the rails, insert screws, and tighten.

If the door still sags, attach two T-braces as shown and connect them with a light steel cable. Install a turnbuckle near one corner to pull the wire tight and keep it that way.

SOLVING WINDOW PROBLEMS

Like malfunctioning doors, windows that don't work properly are easy to ignore. In many cases, the repairs needed to restore the window to normal operation are simple and inexpensive.

Unsticking a Double-Hung Window

Of the many varieties of windows, the centuries-old double-hung style is the most prone to trouble, particularly sticking. There are two basic reasons for this. Dirt or paint has worked into the channels, or the sash and the frame have swollen in damp weather.

If the window simply won't open, start by working a stiff putty knife (not a screwdriver, which will gouge the wood) all the way around between the sash and the stops. Do it both inside and outside, breaking away any paint that may have sealed the window shut. Use a hammer to tap the putty knife in firmly and work it back and forth to loosen the window.

If the window still will not move, tap a hatchet blade or a metal wedge between the bottom of the sash and the sill from the outside. Work slowly across the base of the window so that the sash moves upward evenly and doesn't bind.

Once you have opened the window, scrape away any loose paint and clean the pulley stiles, or window channels, thoroughly. This area can be lubricated with a silicone spray, paraffin, or wax.

If the window still doesn't move freely, it may be that the wood in the sash and the stops has swollen, causing it to bind. One way to correct this is to cut a 6-inch length of wood that fits snugly into the channel. Hammer it in at various points to widen the channel slightly. The stops should spread enough to let the sash move freely.

If this still doesn't solve the problem, the stops and both sashes will have to be removed. For details on that process, see page 100. When the sashes are out, sand or plane both sides evenly until the window moves freely.

Unsticking a Casement Window

Check first to see whether the window has been painted shut. If so, clear it with a putty knife worked between the sash and the frame, as described for the double-hung window.

The most common problem with casements is a stiff adjusting arm. See page 101 for instructions on dealing with this.

Unsticking a Sliding Window

Again, first see whether the window has been painted shut. If so, run a putty knife around the edge of the sash to break it loose, as described for the double-hung window.

More probably, the sticking is caused by debris in the tracks at the bottom. Vacuum the area clean and then lubricate it with paraffin or a silicone spray.

Don't try to pry the window loose with a screwdriver or other such tool. You're more likely to bend the tracks permanently out of line than to correct the sticking.

Repairing a Double-Hung Window

The mechanism of some double-hung windows can be modernized as well as repaired. Sash cords, which tend to break and tangle, can be replaced with chains or with spring balances. Spring lifts can be adjusted to give the correct amount of tension.

Freeing a Stuck Window

Start with a putty knife

Use a wedge or hatchet blade if necessary

Clean channels thoroughly

Tap wood block into channels

Lubricate channels

Fixing Window Mechanisms

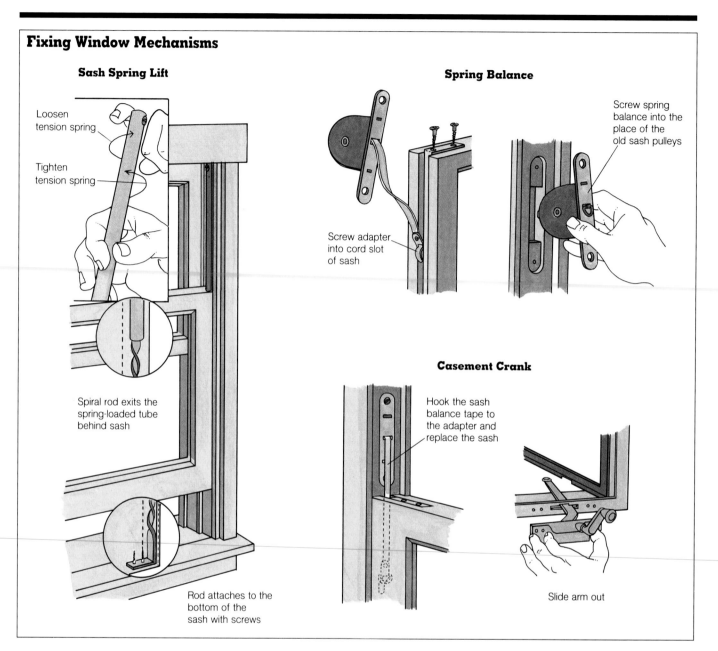

Sash Spring Lift

Loosen tension spring

Tighten tension spring

Spiral rod exits the spring-loaded tube behind sash

Rod attaches to the bottom of the sash with screws

Spring Balance

Screw adapter into cord slot of sash

Screw spring balance into the place of the old sash pulleys

Casement Crank

Hook the sash balance tape to the adapter and replace the sash

Slide arm out

Replacing a Sash Cord

Start by removing the stop along the side that has the broken or tangled sash cord. It may be screwed in place. If it is not, loosen it with a chisel or a flat prybar, working from inside the channel if possible to minimize damage.

Once the stop molding for the lower sash has been removed, ease the sash out of the frame just enough to free the knotted end of the cord from the sash groove. Lower the weight gently and let the knot rest against the pulley.

To get at the weight, there may be a small access panel at the bottom of the channel. If it has never been removed, you may not be able to see it under the paint. Search out the panel with a nail or awl; then find the one or two nails or screws that hold it in place. In very old houses this panel may never have been cut completely through, and you will have to finish the job, using a drill and a keyhole saw. If there is no access panel, you will have to remove the side of the window casing to reach the weight.

Note that even if it is the upper sash cord that needs repair, you still must first remove the lower sash. To remove the upper sash, pull out the parting strip between the two sashes. Slide the upper window down as far as it will go. Starting from the top, pull the strip out of its groove with a pair of pliers. Sometimes it has been screwed or nailed in place, so check before pulling.

Use a protective piece of wood on each side of the parting strip so that it won't be damaged by the pliers. The upper sash cord and weight are removed in the same manner as the lower ones.

Sash cords should be replaced with chains, which require no maintenance. Drop the chain down the channel and then run it through the hole at the top of the weight. Secure the weight to the chain with wire.

Now put the sash back in place as if it were fully closed. For the lower window raise the sash weight until it is just below the sash pulley. For the upper window the weight should be about 2 inches from the bottom of the window opening. When you have adjusted the weight, fasten the chain securely to the sash by inserting two screws through the links. Make sure that the screw heads do not protrude beyond the slot.

Before you reinstall the panel cover and the stops, make sure that the window works smoothly.

Adjusting a Spring Lift

You can spot this device by the metal tube that runs up the window casing channel. It eliminates the need for sash cords and weights, and it can be tightened or loosened to adjust the movement of the window.

If the window tends to creep up after it has been opened, the spring is too tight. To loosen the spring remove the tube at the top of the window and let the screw unwind two or three turns to the left. Keep firm control of the screw. If the window does not move easily, give the screw a couple of turns to the right to increase the tension.

Replacing a Spring Balance

This device can easily be installed to replace the sash cords and weights. Built something like a self-retracting steel measuring tape, it is designed to fit into the opening for the pulleys on a double-hung window frame. An adapter hooks the tape to the sash. Sash balances come in kits; the different sizes fit different sizes of window. The chart that accompanies the kit will tell you which size to buy.

Repairing a Casement Window

Some casements are opened and shut by means of a simple sliding rod. Clean these rods and occasionally lubricate them with powdered graphite.

Most modern casement windows have a cranking mechanism. When repairs are necessary check the gears first. To do this loosen the setscrew on the handle and remove it. Then remove the two screws holding the gear box to the side of the window frame. Finally, remove the arm by sliding it along the slot until it lifts free. In some cases, you will have to unscrew the hinged fitting that holds it in place.

Inspect the gears carefully. If they are dirty clean them with solvent that won't damage the metal, then apply fresh grease. Never use gasoline for cleaning; it's a fire hazard. If the gears are worn and are not meshing smoothly, the whole mechanism will have to be replaced. Large hardware stores, or lumberyards that sell casement windows can order one for you if they don't have it in

stock. Take the old mechanism with you to ensure that you order a new one of the right size.

For casement windows that do not close tightly enough, you can shim behind the locking handle. Just remove it and slip a shim under the plate. The handle, when it is reinstalled,

will now draw the window sash up snug against the frame.

Repairing a Sliding Window

Sliding windows are largely maintenance free as long as the channel in which they slide is kept clean. If one of the rails is bent, correct it as you would for a sliding door (see page 98).

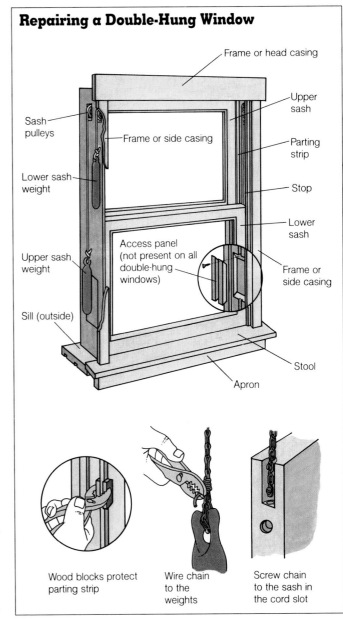

Repairing a Double-Hung Window

Frame or head casing

Sash pulleys

Frame or side casing

Lower sash weight

Upper sash weight

Sill (outside)

Access panel (not present on all double-hung windows)

Apron

Upper sash

Parting strip

Stop

Lower sash

Frame or side casing

Stool

Wood blocks protect parting strip

Wire chain to the weights

Screw chain to the sash in the cord slot

REPAINTING DOORS AND WINDOWS

Repainting wood doors and windows, especially if you first have to remove the old paint, is a hard, tedious job. However, it improves the appearance and life of the doors and windows so much that it is worth it.

Preparing Wood for Painting

If the paint on the frame is in reasonably good shape, go over it carefully for blisters. If you find any, scrape them away and sand the area around them smooth. Lightly sand the paint on the sash and frame; then wipe it clean.

If the paint is in poor condition—cracked and peeling—it must be removed. Simply painting over it will not do because the new paint will not adhere to the old.

The best tool for wide, flat surfaces is a pull scraper, available at hardware stores. For narrow areas use a flat-blade scraper. An easier, albeit more expensive, way is to use paint remover. Brush it on, wait until the paint is softened, and then peel it off with a putty knife. Any tough spots that remain must be scraped.

After most of the old paint is off, sand the frame and sash with a coarse (80-grit) sandpaper to remove the stubborn flakes. Then go over it again with a fine (180-grit) paper. Always sand with the grain of the wood. Finally, go over the frame with a damp cloth to remove all the sanding particles.

If there are any gouges in the wood, fill them in now with wood putty or patching compound. Wood putty is applied directly from the can. Patching compound—a dry powder—is first mixed with water to the consistency of thick cream. If the gouge is more than ⅛ inch deep, fill it with two separate coats to prevent shrinkage. Use a putty knife to apply the filler, and sand each coat after it is dry.

Repainting Doors

When you repaint a door, apply primer, then a finish coat. The easiest way to paint a door is to take it off its hinges. Prop it against a wall or lay it across two sawhorses. Do not remove the hinges but cover them with masking tape. If you are using oil-based paint, first lay it on with a roller, then spread it with a brush as described below. If it's latex paint, use a brush for the whole process.

First, using a roller, cover the door as well as you can. Work out from the middle, first up and then down. If the door is paneled, do the panels first.

Immediately after rolling, spread and even out the paint with a 2-inch trim brush, following the grain of the wood. If the door is paneled, begin with the panels, painting the molding that frames them first. "Pull out" paint from inside corners by working the brush into the corner and pulling it out and away from the surface.

The latch edge of the door should match the room it opens into; the hinge edge should match the room it opens away from. Paint all the edges. Paint the frame, working downward from the top. Consult the illustration to determine how much of the stop to paint.

Repainting Windows

Two coats of paint should always be applied to windows—first the primer coat, which will seal the wood and make the finish coat adhere and then

---

Painting a Door

Work out from the middle

"Pulling out" paint from corners

Stop

the finish coat itself. The techniques described below are the same for both. With latex paint use latex primer; use an oil-based primer with oil-based paint. Latex paint is very popular today for use on houses because its quality is high, it cleans up with soap and water, and it is cheaper than oil-based paints.

Be sure to choose the right brush. For latex paint use only synthetic bristles. Natural bristles, which are stiff hairs from a hog, should be used only for oil-based paints. For window sashes and frames, a 3-inch-wide brush is usually sufficient. Buy the best; it will hold more paint, and fewer bristles will fall out and stick on the newly painted surface. On a good finish brush, the bristles are feathered (not all the same length) rather than cut square at the end. This allows you to press the brush down and paint a fine, clean edge.

Before you start to paint, cover the glass along the edge of the sash with strips of masking, transparent, or painter's tape, leaving 1/16 inch of glass exposed. This allows the paint to form a complete, watertight seal over the window putty. Since it is difficult to leave such a narrow margin at the corners, apply the tape flush with the edge of the sash and then cut away a 1/16-inch margin with a utility knife. Remove the tape immediately after the paint sets.

Double-Hung Windows

To paint a double-hung window, first raise the inner sash about 12 inches. Lower the outer sash enough to expose the top 6 inches of the inner sash. Working from the outside,

Painting a Double-Hung Window

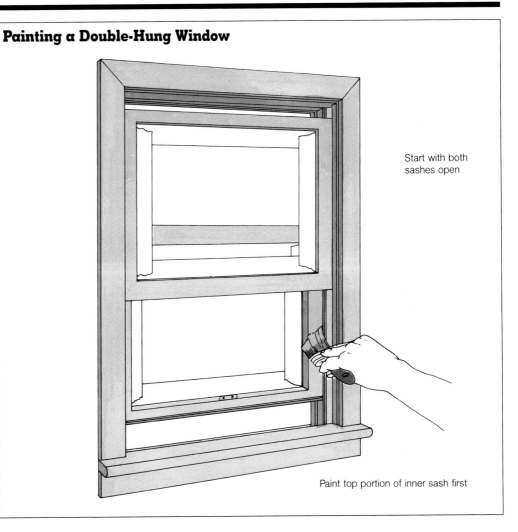

Start with both sashes open

Paint top portion of inner sash first

paint those exposed 6 inches, starting at the top and working down. Next, paint the outer sash, including the bottom edge. Close both windows all but about 2 inches and finish painting the inner sash. Do not close the window fully until the paint is completely dry. Move both sashes a few inches several times during the drying period to prevent sticking.

After you have painted both sashes, paint the casing and trim, again working from top to bottom so that you can pick up any drips and drops as you go.

The inside is painted in the same way as the outside. Remove all the hardware first.

Casement Windows

Start by removing all of the hardware except the hinges. Now apply masking tape. For a neat job around hinges, cover them with tape and cut around the edges with a utility knife. The window is then painted in a straightforward fashion.

Painting Steel and Aluminum

Steel windows must be kept painted to prevent them from rusting. Aluminum windows are not normally painted, but they can be finished with a

protective coat of urethane if pitting is a problem in your area.

Steel windows should be sanded to bare metal before painting. A tough emery cloth works well here. Next, wash down the steel with white vinegar. This cleans it and also helps the paint to adhere. When the frame is dry, apply a coat of metal primer. Then put on a finish coat of paint formulated for metal, which is usually oil based. Be careful not to get paint into the gear mechanism.

Most metal doors have a baked-enamel finish that should not require attention. You can touch up any chips with a matching metal enamel paint.

SEALING THE HOUSE

The best conservation method can also be the simplest: Make sure that all of the door and window openings in the house are tightly sealed.

Reducing Heat Loss Through Windows

The windows in newer homes are often made with double-pane glass. This is the best method of reducing heat loss through windows. If you wish to install double-pane glass, you will have to replace the whole window; turn to pages 58 to 61 for instructions. If, however, you're not ready to replace single-pane windows, there are some other approaches that you can try.

Storm Windows

These work by creating a dead-air space, just as thermal windows do. For storm windows to function efficiently, there must be no gaps between the frames of the existing windows and the wall coverings, but there must be weep holes in the storm window frame to release condensation.

The type of storm window you use will depend in part on the type of window you have. For instance, some sliding aluminum-framed models have interchangeable storm windows that slip into channels around the outside of the unit. Other storm windows can be made to order at custom shops to fit directly over the existing windows. They have weather stripping around the interior edges, and they are simply screwed or snapped into place.

Storm doors should be made up in custom shops, for they must fit the door opening exactly. If any air leaks in around the edges, much of their energy-saving value is lost.

Plastic Sheeting

A less attractive but cheaper storm window can be made by simply stretching sheets of polyethylene across the outside of the existing window. This material is available at most hardware stores. However, it is not perfectly transparent, so visibility will be reduced. It is suitable only for installations where the view is secondary.

To cover the window, cut 4-mil or 6-mil polyethylene sheeting so that it is 2 inches larger than the exterior window frame. Fold under 1 inch and staple the double edge to the top of the frame. Cover the plastic with a length of lath cut to fit, and tack it in place. Repeat the process for the bottom and then the sides. Run a bead of caulk around the outside of the lath to seal it.

To cover windows that you wish to see out of, there is a plastic-film insulation kit. Working on the inside of the window, simply tape the film around the frame and then go over it with an electric hair dryer. The heat shrinks the plastic to a wrinkle-free, clear covering. One package has enough material to cover five 3-foot by 5-foot windows.

You can also screw a sheet of acrylic plastic over the window.

Reducing Heat Gain Through Windows

Windows can bring in too much direct radiant heat from the sun. One way to reduce heat gain is to cover the windows with a reflective film. Another way is to install solar screens. These are placed on the outside, much like storm

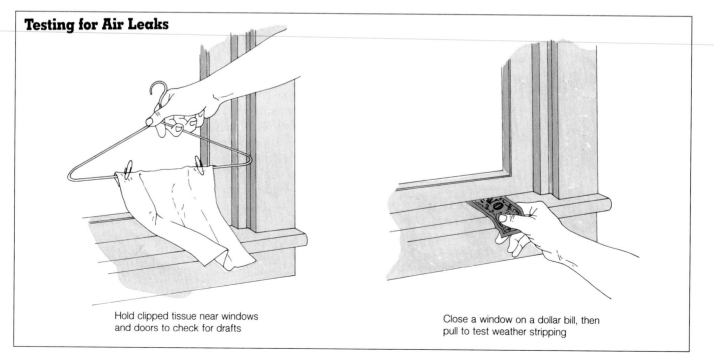

Testing for Air Leaks

Hold clipped tissue near windows and doors to check for drafts

Close a window on a dollar bill, then pull to test weather stripping

Weather-Stripping Materials

Weather stripping is used around doors and around windows that must open and shut. It is generally made of metal or rubber. There are so many different types of weather stripping that you may feel defeated before you start when it comes to choosing one. Here is a selection of weather-stripping materials together with advice on where to use each kind.

Felt Strip

Inexpensive; made of hair, wool, or polyester. Tack or glue around double-hung windows.

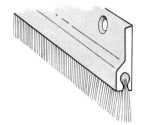

Foam Tape

Made of polyurethane or vinyl, it's easy to apply. Self-adhering. Use on double-hung windows or on side casing for sliding glass door.

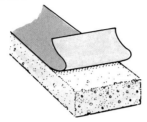

Sponge Rubber

Made of neoprene; somewhat harder and longer lasting than either felt strip or foam tape. Use in same manner.

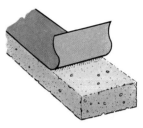

Flange Stripping

Made of vinyl or rubber. The flat part is tacked to the door or window jamb and the bulb is compressed when the unit is closed.

Tension Strip

Made of metal or vinyl, widely considered the most effective and longest lasting weather stripping. More expensive than others. Vinyl has self-sticking surface. Metal is more difficult to install. Available in colors.

Door Sweep

Simple and effective. The metal or plastic top section is screwed to the inside of the door. Slot allows fine adjustment. The vinyl sweep will catch on a carpet but is an excellent choice over hardwood floors. Adjustable type screws to the outside of the door; spring mechanism raises it above carpet.

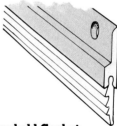

Bristle Sweep

This device with nylon bristles in a metal or plastic retainer is a good choice under sliding glass doors.

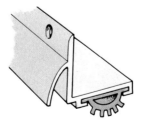

Door Shoe

This device is very effective. The metal shoe with a drip edge to block blowing rain is screwed to exterior of door and then vinyl strip is inserted. Careful trimming of the door is required for a perfect fit.

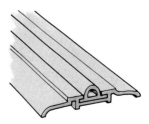

Threshold Gasket

This weather stripping is built into the threshold instead of into the door. You will have to remove the door to screw the device into the existing threshold. The door must then be carefully measured and cut for precise fit.

Installing Door Weather Stripping

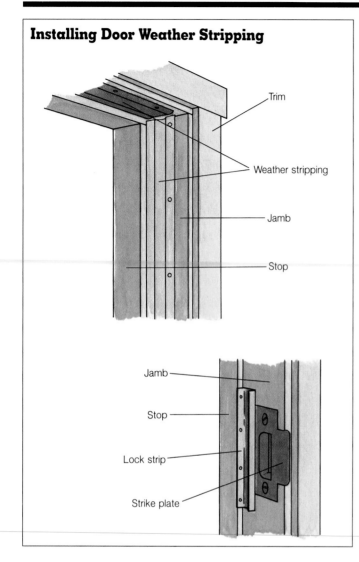

Trim

Weather stripping

Jamb

Stop

Jamb

Stop

Lock strip

Strike plate

draft will cause the tissue to flutter. Do the same around air conditioners, or around stove and clothes-dryer vents where they pass through walls. You can also do the test with a lighted cigarette, watching the movement of the smoke.

Place a dollar bill across the weather stripping of a window and then close the window. If you can pull out the dollar bill with little or no resistance, the weather stripping is insufficient.

Most drafts enter the house through doors and windows. These are the most important parts of the house to seal off.

Caulking

Caulk is a puttylike substance used to seal cracks where air might enter the house. Caulk is also commonly used around the exterior trim of doors and windows to keep moisture out. It is most widely sold in standard-sized cartridges, but it also comes in toothpaste-sized dispensers for small cracks. In addition, you can buy it in coils for cracks ½ inch or wider. Good caulk remains elastic for three to ten years, depending on its quality.

The problem in choosing caulk is deciding which product is best for your needs. For a discussion of caulking materials, refer to page 35.

Interiors

Door and window frames should be caulked on the inside during installation. Large gaps around windows and doors should be loosely filled with insulation, and smaller gaps

should be caulked before the interior trim is put in place. If you are not sure whether this has been done, do not attempt to remove the interior trim boards. They are tightly nailed, and you will probably split them or damage the wall. Instead, weather-strip the window or door and caulk around the exterior trim.

Exteriors

Check the caulk (if there is any) where the door or window trim meets the house siding. Don't forget the trim on top. If the existing caulk is cracked, broken, or dried out, use a chisel to remove all of it. Choose a caulk of a matching color and apply a bead to fill all the gaps.

Weather-Stripping a Door

You can weather-strip most doors by following the instructions for weather-stripping a window (see pages 108 and 109). Although most doors are larger than windows, they are generally easier to weather-strip because they don't have double sashes and center bars.

Whatever method you use, first measure the weather stripping carefully against the frame of the door. Then seat it onto the frame against the doorstop so that it fits tightly when the door is shut, but not so tightly that the door can't close. To ensure a proper fit, you may want to tack the stripping loosely into place first and test it by opening and shutting the door gently a few times. Then you can drive the nails and set the heads.

windows. They will cut glare by 20 to 70 percent, depending on the weave of the screen. Visibility is not greatly impaired.

Some double-pane windows have miniblinds set between the panes. They can be adjusted to control the amount of sunlight passing through.

Finally, don't forget the old standby of simply hanging a bamboo or vinyl roll-up screen from the eaves.

Filling the Gaps

You will be pleasantly surprised at the changes you can make with a few hours' work at caulking and weather-stripping. Stopping the flow of air into a house will also make that house much cleaner.

Even if you think you have a fairly airtight house, try some of these tests (see page 104). On a breezy day clip the edge of a tissue square to a hanger and then hold it at various points around the edges of the doors and windows. Even a faint

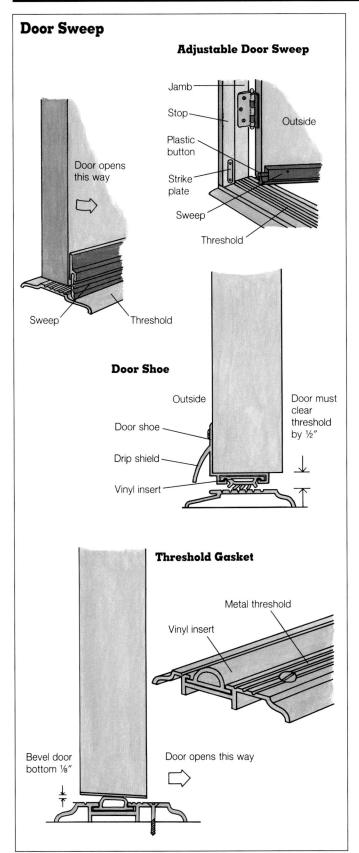

Door Sweep

Adjustable Door Sweep

Jamb
Stop
Plastic button
Strike plate
Sweep
Threshold
Outside
Door opens this way
Sweep
Threshold

Door Shoe

Outside
Door shoe
Drip shield
Vinyl insert
Door must clear threshold by ½"

Threshold Gasket

Metal threshold
Vinyl insert
Bevel door bottom ⅛"
Door opens this way

The exterior door is a major source of drafts. Its opening is extremely large, and the weight of the door swinging on its hinges over many years tends to loosen the screws and cause the door to sag, making its edge meet the jambs unevenly. It's definitely worth your while to weather-strip an exterior door, even though it isn't always easy.

If the door hangs unevenly, you may have to remove it from its hinges and rehang it (see pages 94 and 95). Otherwise the seal between the door and the stripping may not be tight. While the door is off, you may want to trim the bottom to accommodate a door shoe or a threshold gasket. These are both extremely useful devices for keeping out drafts.

Applying the Weather Stripping

Begin with the lock strip, the small piece of stripping provided with most kits. Because this piece is the same height as, and placed behind, the strike plate, it will help to guide you in measuring and placing the weather stripping on the latch side of the jamb.

When the lock strip is in place, complete the stripping on the sides and top of the jamb, keeping the flanges facing toward the doorstop. The bottom of the door will be stripped in another fashion.

Weather-Stripping the Bottom of a Door

Of course, since cold air falls, it is most likely to enter your home through the lowest available cracks. Virtually any house is subject to this kind of infiltration at the bottoms of exterior doors.

There are various ways to plug these door-bottom cracks. All methods entail either lowering the bottom of the door or raising the top of the threshold.

The most common and effective kinds of weather stripping you can add to the bottoms of doors are the door sweep, the door shoe, and the threshold gasket.

Door Sweep

The simplest door-bottom, weather stripping is a sweep made of vinyl or bristle that is easily attached while the door is on its hinges. Just cut the sweep to size and screw it to the base of the door in a position that allows the door to open and close easily.

Adjustable door sweeps raise up when you open the door inward (over carpeting, for example) and lower back down when you close the door, creating a tight seal. The adjustable sweep is surface mounted to the outside face of the door. To attach it close the door and measure the width between the stops. Cut the sweep to this size with a hacksaw. While you cut, hold the movable part of the sweep in the *up* position; be sure not to cut the end with the plastic button. Screw the sweep to the door with the door closed. Hold the sweep in the *down* position; the rubber bottom must be on the hinge side of the door and pressed snugly against the threshold. Note where the plastic button hits the stop. Open the door and nail the little strike plate that comes with the sweep into position at this spot.

Door Shoe

This device resembles an adjustable door sweep, but it doesn't "sweep." Instead, the vinyl ridges of its tubular gasket make a tight seal with the doorsill or the threshold.

Attach a door shoe as you would an adjustable door sweep, gauging its fit as you work and trimming it with a hacksaw if necessary. Remove the curved vinyl ridge from the shoe, slide the shoe over the bottom of the doors, screw it on securely, and replace the vinyl so that it makes a tight seal with the threshold.

Threshold Gasket

If you intend to attach a door shoe, the threshold must be in fairly good condition, and it should preferably be made of wood, so that the ridges of the gasket can grasp and make a tight seal. If you have no threshold, or if yours is worn enough to be replaced, consider installing a threshold gasket, as well as door-bottom weather stripping. The disadvantage of a threshold gasket is that it gets walked on and eventually wears out.

To attach any threshold, it is often necessary to remove the door from its hinges in order to gain complete access to the threshold area. You may also have to trim the bottom of the door to accommodate the added height of the threshold. If so, first be sure to measure the sill, the door bottom, and the new threshold carefully, so that you know exactly how much of which part you must trim. If you trim too much from the door bottom, you will defeat the purpose of the weather stripping; if you do not trim

enough, the new gasket will wear out very quickly.

If you must trim the door, do it before you trim the threshold. Then cut the threshold to the proper width with a hacksaw, and file it smooth. Center the threshold and screw it into place.

In any case, to achieve a tight seal, you may have to remove the door and bevel its base about ⅛ inch against the vinyl. Do not bevel in the wrong direction, or you may find it impossible to open the door.

Weather-Stripping a Window

Every window, like every kind of stripping, has its own peculiarities, so use these recommendations as general guidelines, and follow the instructions provided by the manufacturer of the weather stripping you select.

Weather stripping is only appropriate for windows that open. Fixed-pane and greenhouse windows and skylights should be caulked and do not require weather stripping. Jalousie windows cannot be fully sealed, so they are recommended only for warm climates or for porches attached to properly sealed houses.

The combination of the double-hung sash and metal tension stripping shown here allows for the most complete explanation of the procedure of weather-stripping a window. Like all weather stripping, metal strips should be installed with the resilient face pressing against the sash tightly enough to make a good seal but not so tightly that the window will stick.

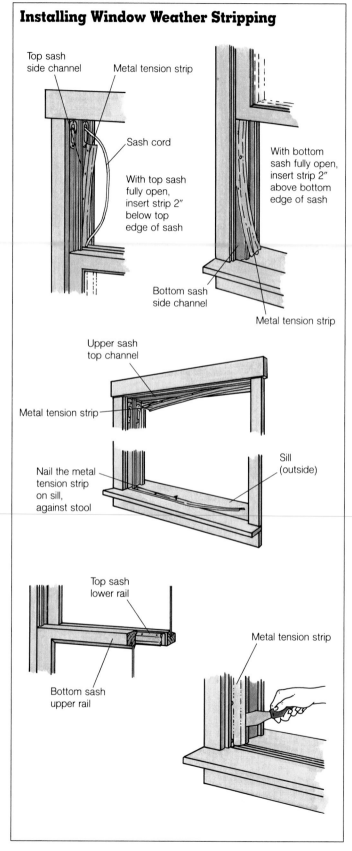

Installing Window Weather Stripping

Top sash side channel

Metal tension strip

Sash cord

With top sash fully open, insert strip 2" below top edge of sash

With bottom sash fully open, insert strip 2" above bottom edge of sash

Bottom sash side channel

Metal tension strip

Upper sash top channel

Metal tension strip

Nail the metal tension strip on sill, against stool

Sill (outside)

Top sash lower rail

Bottom sash upper rail

Metal tension strip

Installing Window Weather Stripping

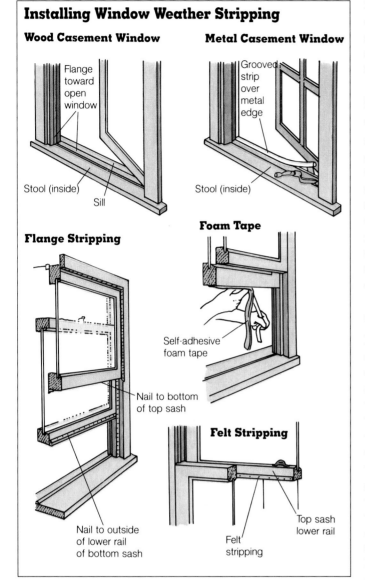

Wood Casement Window

Flange toward open window

Stool (inside)

Sill

Metal Casement Window

Grooved strip over metal edge

Stool (inside)

Flange Stripping

Nail to bottom of top sash

Nail to outside of lower rail of bottom sash

Foam Tape

Self-adhesive foam tape

Felt Stripping

Felt stripping

Top sash lower rail

Double-Hung Window

Measure strips to fit the side channels for both sashes, as well as the upper rail of the top sash, the lower rail of the bottom sash, and the lower rail of the top sash (the center bar). Cut the strips with tin snips.

Slide the side channel strips into place between the sashes and jambs and nail them down. Be careful not to cover the mechanisms in the tops of the channels.

Slide the upper-rail top-sash strip into the top channel of the window and the lower-rail bottom-sash strip into the bottom channel. Nail them in place. Alternatively, you can nail the upper-rail top-sash strip to the upper side of the top sash and the lower-rail bottom-sash strip to the underside of the bottom sash.

Nail the last strip to the inside surface of the lower rail of the top sash (the center bar).

If the strips don't fit tightly enough, you can pry out the side-channel flanges with a screwdriver or a putty knife. Set all nails to prevent snagging.

Sliding Window

This is weather-stripped in the same way as a double-hung sash window—just imagine that it's lying on its side. If only one sash slides, use metal tension stripping in the channel that opens and seal the three remaining edges of the movable sash with tubular flange stripping to create a good seal all the way around.

Casement Window

For a wood casement window, a rotating window, or any kind of tilting window, such as an awning or a hopper, nail the weather stripping to the frame with the flange along the edge toward which the window opens. For a metal casement window, buy a deeply grooved gasket stripping that can be fitted over all the metal edges of the window frame. (This is available at most hardware stores.) To make the stripping hold better, first apply a rubber/metal or a vinyl/metal glue to the edge of the frame or to the gasket channel.

Alternate Methods

Different types of weather stripping require different installation methods. Some of these methods are discussed below.

Flange Stripping

Vinyl or rubber stripping can simply be tacked all around the sash. If you nail it to the outside of the window frame, it will be less visible, but inside or out, it should fit tightly on all surfaces, including the lower rail of the top sash. Nail gasket stripping to the window frame with the thick or bulbous side against the sash. Make sure that the rolled edges fit tightly against the window when it's closed. Then add stripping to the lower rail of the top sash (the center bar) on the inside edge, to make a tight seal between the sashes when the whole window is closed. Make sure to strip all of the edges of the window.

Foam Tape and Sponge Rubber

Any adhesive-backed stripping can simply be pressed into place with your fingers. Clean the surface so that the tape will adhere. Then apply the stripping, slowly pulling off the paper or plastic backing as you go. Do not use this type of weather stripping where it will encounter friction—for example, in side channels. It will wear out quickly or even pull right off.

Felt Stripping

To install felt, you can either staple it in place with an ordinary heavy-duty stapler or nail it to the window frame like gasket stripping. Add a length of felt to the inside of the lower rail of the top sash to block infiltration between the sashes. Don't attach felt stripping to the outside of a window where it is liable to get wet, because it may rot. Like foam tape, felt should not be used where it will encounter friction.

INDEX

U.S./Metric Measure Conversion Chart

		Formulas for Exact Measures			Rounded Measures for Quick Reference		
	Symbol	**When you know:**	**Multiply by:**	**To find:**			
Mass (Weight)	oz	ounces	28.35	grams	1 oz		= 30 g
	lb	pounds	0.45	kilograms	4 oz		= 115 g
	g	grams	0.035	ounces	8 oz		= 225 g
	kg	kilograms	2.2	pounds	16 oz	= 1 lb	= 450 g
					32 oz	= 2 lb	= 900 g
					36 oz	= 2¼ lb	= 1000 g (1 kg)
Volume	tsp	teaspoons	5.0	milliliters	¼ tsp	= 1/24 oz	= 1 ml
	tbsp	tablespoons	15.0	milliliters	½ tsp	= 1/12 oz	= 2 ml
	fl oz	fluid ounces	29.57	milliliters	1 tsp	= 1/6 oz	= 5 ml
	c	cups	0.24	liters	1 tbsp	= ½ oz	= 15 ml
	pt	pints	0.47	liters	1 c	= 8 oz	= 250 ml
	qt	quarts	0.95	liters	2 c (1 pt)	= 16 oz	= 500 ml
	gal	gallons	3.785	liters	4 c (1 qt)	= 32 oz	= 1 liter
	ml	milliliters	0.034	fluid ounces	4 qt (1 gal)	= 128 oz	= 3¾ liter
Length	in.	inches	2.54	centimeters	⅜ in.	= 1 cm	
	ft	feet	30.48	centimeters	1 in.	= 2.5 cm	
	yd	yards	0.9144	meters	2 in.	= 5 cm	
	mi	miles	1.609	kilometers	2½ in.	= 6.5 cm	
	km	kilometers	0.621	miles	12 in. (1 ft)	= 30 cm	
	m	meters	1.094	yards	1 yd	= 90 cm	
	cm	centimeters	0.39	inches	100 ft	= 30 m	
					1 mi	= 1.6 km	
Temperature	° F	Fahrenheit	5/9 (after subtracting 32)	Celsius	32° F	= 0° C	
					68°F	= 20°C	
	° C	Celsius	9/5 (then add 32)	Fahrenheit	212° F	= 100° C	
Area	in.^{2}	square inches	6.452	square centimeters	1 in.^{2}	= 6.5 cm^2	
	ft^2	square feet	929.0	square centimeters	1 ft^2	= 930 cm^2	
	yd^2	square yards	8361.0	square centimeters	1 yd^2	= 8360 cm^2	
	a.	acres	0.4047	hectares	1 a.	= 4050 m^2	